THE MALTESE JORDANS

JOIN THE FAMILY

Want free stuff? Join my Palms Family!

At the end of this book, you'll find a page telling you how to sign up for my author newsletter. Follow the link to join and I'll send you another book in the series for FREE!

From there, you'll get updates about new releases, special content, info on my street team and audio podcasts, and much, much more!

Thanks for reading!

JACK PALMS IN
THE MALTESE JORDANS

SETH HARWOOD

CrimeWAV Books

ISBN-10: 1-948235-97-8
ISBN-13: 978-1-948235-97-6

Acknowledgments

Thank you to all of my subscribers on Patreon. Your support means so much!

Thanks to the first wave—people who came right in: Mike Dunham, Mike Bennett, Paul Crowe, Adell Barnes, Dale Bennett, David Heyes, Alasdair Sanderson, Chris McGilvray, Stephen Jacob, Elliott Kolner, Asher Samuels, Ann Marie Smith, Ernie Pyle, Chris Pragman, Ian Gregg, Joel Gerhold, Seth Strong.

Thanks to Steve Owens, my boy Squeaky Clean. You're in a class by yourself.

Thanks to Carlos "Chicago" Mendoza, Doug Farrow, Kimberly Ewertz, Josh Meyer, Jennifer Hathorne, Arioch Morningstar, Kate Sherrod, Simon Monk, Tim Tharp, David Aimerito, Tim and Kevin Hesselton (two fine Sn'eads), Jim Blanas, Rob Stauffer, David Washington, Deborah Szajngarten, John Bivins, Cameron Mathews, Garion Lopez, Martin McIntosh, Jeanine Terranella, David Jacobs, Maria Alejandro, Paul Lewis, Amy Bykerk, and Slava Morozov.

Thanks to Jesse Simonin, Didier Sicaud, Michael Kimberlin, Scott and Maegan Breakall, Rich Katz, Paul Motsuk, Richard Dubya, Mark Coggins, Mark Solocinski, Daniel Ritchie, John Mierau, Ray Sylvester, Dwight Dunlop, Robb Olson, Harley Mazuk, Eve Mitchell, Ed Parrot, Paul E Cooley, Marj Snyder, Ronald Krueger, Christopher Young, Eric Meaders, David De Zwirek, Andrew Roland, and Boysen Hodgson.

For the helpers whose work I can never repay, thanks to Jason Andrews, Mike Farley, Steve Riekeberg, and Lee Dal Monte.

Thanks for the support of my wonderful students and writers: Richard Ferri, Victoria Ferenbach, Bennett Gates, Erika Rich, Jeannie Hua Ferguson, Lura Seavey, Connie Howard, Nell Porter Brown, Brett Welch, and Liz Coleman.

Thanks to my family: Mom, Dad, Gogo, Jess, Maggie, Nana and Jim, Grampa Bruce, Aunt Sheila and her whole crew, Palms Uncle Stu Cohen and Connie, Ruth and Stan, and everyone else. You know who you are. I love you.

For Kelly and Willa, all my heart. You are my girls, my rock, my foundation.

Part I

The Runner

I'll kill you if you try me for my Air Max 95s.

1

Late Lunch

The Bay Area
Northern California
January, 2014
The Golden State Warriors have not won a title since 1975. Barack
Obama is president of the United States.

It wasn't long before the bail bondsmen called. Once they heard I was hunting people they got after me to do their jobs. If you've done any chasing, you're bound to get a call when they're desperate, which is most of the time.

It was enough I'd worked with Mills Hopkins, helped the SFPD and touched bases with the Feds. These got me into their system. Call it a database. Radar. Call it whatever you like, it meant I was getting phone calls. Invitations. Even without having my license. They didn't care. Dog the Bounty Hunter had people crazy, thinking anyone tough could do the job, and somehow in people's minds I fit that bill. Thanks again to *Shake 'Em Down.*

When the bounty was high enough, or I needed the cash, I took a job.

This one was different. Sure, the money was right, that was part of it, but the bigger part was the mark. This runner, he was from Hawaii and headed home.

I was thinking hard on this, chewing a straw, listening on my end of the phone to Joe Leonardi. A club soda sat on my table next to a Shrimp Louie salad I hadn't touched, all this at my favorite bar in Sausalito, looking out over the marina. The sun shone down on the bay, and I shivered a little in my coat as a mid-January breeze blew in.

Joe Leonardi was the bondsman who had the ticket for a million-dollar bond. And this mark was no idiot, according to Joe.

"He's a real Fucking Genius. Certified F.G. That's why I called you, Jack. This job needs your wits and particular set of capabilities."

"You tell that to the other five guys you called first?"

"You know I did." He laughed, ever the charmer. "But they aren't my favorite action movie star, are they? You know what I'm talking about. Eh, Jack? Jackie boy."

I grunted in the positive. I'd heard his flattery before; I was either great at what I did, somebody's favorite actor, or the man-candy a guy's wife lusted after. None of the possibilities added motivation. It was all about money. I cared how much I'd be paid and how badly I needed it.

Right then, I could use it pretty bad. Mortgage was up and the Mustang needed a new suspension.

Joe kept on about his guy, this mark called Meyer Mody.

"A real shyster," he was saying. "Embezzled into eight figures from his firm. White-collar crime. Smartass goes down, he spends a few years in a flipping country club, but this dickhead runs. His people all in Hawaii. That make you want to help?"

It did. Truth was, this was the best thing Joe had said so far.

I knew I was soft to think of any month in the Bay Area as real winter, but anyone I knew had just gotten back from someplace—skiing or warm shores. Thoughts of escape were kicking around in my head. My old East Coast self would've vomited in shame at the thought of running from a winter as mild as the Bay Area's—sixty degree days and hardly any rain in recent years—but there it was. Just a mention of Hawaii turned me on.

"So why not?" he said. "Or are you even still there, you fucking piece-of-shit has-been?"

"Whoa, big fella. Easy now."

"He speaks. Thought I'd lost you."

"Maybe you just did."

"Let's not break balls. You want this or don't you? Pays an even fifty."

"Seventy-five."

"Sixty."

That was all he had to say. I needed money and sixty large filled the hole. "Done. Email me the deets."

I hung up, paying him back for his shot below the belt. Sure, I couldn't get pissy about anyone using the truth of my long-lost acting career to get my attention, but I didn't have to like it, either.

2

Time Capsule

After lunch I read Joe's email and saw the first thing to go my way: Mody's details included an address in Tiburon, just across the water. Not more than a fifteen-minute drive. I looked across the water at the pretty houses, wondering which one was his.

I paid the tab, saving the receipt to bill Joe for later. It was now a business lunch. I walked out to the Fastback: my '67 black beauty that had once been cherry-red but wasn't anymore. I considered its new color a mirror on my soul. Since I'd started dealing with Ralphie and brokering drug deals, the car had taken three bullets and now had a brand-new matte-black paint job, not of my choosing. That's what you get when an ex-black-ops cop with issues tries to do you a favor.

Still, it made me smile every time I saw her: the Fastback, my automotive portrait of Dorian Gray.

The engine roared when I started it, as sure as the weekly time I put in under her hood. Tiburon-bound, I pulled out of the parking lot and headed toward 101.

The guy's address led me to a big house set into a hill along the coast. Sweet views, manicured gardens, windows everywhere. This was a place for a high roller, but just one on a street of many.

Nobody answered when I knocked. If the doorbell worked, I didn't hear it.

I pushed my way through the shrubs and trees, cupping my hands around my eyes as I peered in the window. A brown sectional sofa dominated the living room, situated right in front of a sixty-inch flat screen on the wall. This was a man's place with rented furniture if I'd ever seen one. Taste right out of the Rent-a-Center catalog. Something I knew more than a little about, myself.

It was what I saw below the flat screen, next to the fireplace, that made me smile: an Apple Time Capsule, the kind of wireless router that also acted as a memory storage and backup device.

If this guy had run, he'd taken his computer, but if he'd enabled this Time Capsule and left it behind, then maybe I had just gotten very lucky. It was a lot to ask, but if he'd left this thing with his storage on it, I'd have enough to take a big bite out of his head start.

I saw no security and no wires around the window. You wouldn't exactly call Tiburon trusting, but there were far worse places to live, as far as break-ins went. I slipped the lock on the window using a pen-knife and slid it wide. The window was on a runner about three feet off the ground. Almost like a small sliding door, really. I stepped over the ledge and I was in.

I crossed the living room and crouched down, touched the Time Capsule's cover and felt the warm rumble of little parts humming inside. Its green light was on, so ideally that meant all systems were go. He hadn't even cut the Comcast yet.

I felt around the gadget for its cyber and electrical lifelines, then detached the little animal from its vital supplies. I picked it up and carried it with me as I made my rounds through the house.

There wasn't a lot to be interested in, until I got to the bedroom closet.

This was where I found one of the most impressive sneaker collections I'd ever seen in person. Sure, a few guys in LA had a couple of sweet limited-edition pairs, but this walk-in was like something from *Cribs*. I walked right in, took a deep inhale of the clean leather. That smell, unlike anything else.

This guy Mody had to be crazy, heartbroken, or both—and in grave danger—to leave such a collection behind.

I crouched down, running my finger along the backs of some shoes, mostly Nikes, fingering the rough patterns on some of the soles. Many of these were new-in-box clean. I half wanted to sit and wait here to see what happened to this collection. Runner or not, no matter the bail, you did not construct a closet like this without a whole lot of love. It was not something you'd leave behind. Sooner or later, someone would be back to get this for Mody.

On the other hand, that might take days, so I put my money on the Time Capsule. If that didn't pan out, I liked having a Plan B. I was in no hurry, though; I wanted a good look at these shoes.

What struck me first was the sheer quantity of sneakers. The space was about eight feet by ten feet, a closet made for a couple, but full of sneakers. Custom shelves lined the walls to shoulder height, each of them filled with shoes. They covered the floor and shelves, dominating the small space. Every pair looked brand-new; the whites white and the leather clean. As if he'd scrubbed them with a toothbrush after each wearing. That is, the ones that had even been worn.

I didn't know a whole lot about the various styles, but I knew what I'd seen coming up: shoes that went with certain pro players in given years, memories attached to people I knew who'd worn them. A couple of pairs went with memorable teams: the Michigan Fab Five, Christian Laettner's Duke team, a guy I'd played against in college. Among the few pairs I'd once owned, none was anything fancy.

I didn't know a whole lot about sneakers other than some Adidas, Bird and Magic's Converse Weapons, and Jordan's Nikes. Jordans. There were *a lot* of Air Jordans on the shelves. Jordans from every model year, it seemed, in different patterns and colors. Some models had a whole shelf of variations.

One particular pair of Air Jordans struck me. These were the ones Allen Iverson had worn when he was at Georgetown, back when I was in college myself and couldn't dream of spending that much money on these babies. They had black patent leather running around the base of the shoe and white uppers.

Next to these was the same model in Chicago Bulls colors— black and red—that was all Jordan. Vintage. It was always and would always be Jordan above everyone else. Above everything.

These sneakers had red rubber accent around the soles and the same black patent leather, but were all black from there on up. The logo, the famous silhouette of Jordan jumping, was in red on the side of the ankle. These were *the ones*. If I had to pick a sneaker, one design, one pair, then this was it. My Number One. Holy Grail. Something about their design and shape, their shiny patent leather, it was something no other sneaker ever had. Or could compete with.

I knew some sneakerheads called the Air Max 95 the most

collectible sneaker ever, and I saw a pair of these on Mody's shelf next to some other running shoes, as well as a pretty pair of vintage black Barkleys. But these Jordans, they were my top choice.

Mody had good taste.

In truth, I'd never been much of a collector, though I tried to build a shelf or two when I was making it big in LA. Problem was, at a size 14, not enough of the great sneakers were available in my size. If they'd ever been sold, nobody had them. Not to sell, not to wear, not ever. They just didn't exist. Ghosts, some people called them.

I checked Mody's pair of Jordans knowing they'd be too small. They were size 11.5, standard for collectors and normal-height guys. These would likely have a high resale value and look good on anybody's shelf. Shit, even mine.

I had work to do—to get home and look at Mody's computer files while the trail was still warm—but I couldn't leave this whole collection behind.

I pulled a small duffle bag and stuffed it with the Jordans, the Barkleys and the Air Max 95s. When I walked out of that closet, I had the bag and the Time Capsule. Maybe if nothing else panned out, these three pairs would be enough of a ransom to get Mody to come find me. That, or I'd have a hell of a few old-school display items.

Beyond that, the sneaker closet told me more about Mody than Joe had known: in addition to being an embezzler and a runner, he was likely a pretty good guy on some level. He was a fan and knew a few things about basketball. He also had a real taste for kicks. This guy could definitely qualify as what most people would call a Sneakerhead. A "Sn'ead." And I admired something about that.

3

Ya Mo Be There

Outside Mody's house, I loaded the sneakers into my trunk and headed back to the city, going home to see what the Time Capsule contained.

I was now subletting an apartment out by the beach, on Great Highway, with a view straight out into the Pacific. Nothing to see but horizon and occasionally the Farallons on the clearest of days. San Francisco was that rare coastal city where apartments by the beach were actually affordable. For one, you were way out by the zoo in a no-man's-land, and for another, the fog was on top of you enough of the year that it became unattractive real estate to most. People moved to California to be warm, simple as that.

I had a spot where my kitchen table afforded me a view of the water, a second-floor two-bedroom with moldy rugs and real waves breaking outside my window at night, lulling me to sleep. I couldn't have been happier with it.

When I got inside, I made coffee, laid the gym bag of sneakers gently down on my bed, and set up Mody's Time Capsule on my table, ready to mount it to my laptop. I cracked my knuckles, sat down, and scooted the chair in. There was the ocean, my muse, and the fog was cold enough I still needed my jacket indoors. Compared to Tiburon, I was living low, but it suited me fine.

Turns out Mody's machine, the one backed up on the Time Capsule, was a MacBook Air with a relatively small 64-gigabyte hard drive. For a password, he'd used "Jordans," which was not only taped to the underside of his Time Capsule—a bad security move if there ever was one—but would have been in my top five guesses, regardless. From there I started browsing around as though I had Mody's own computer in my hands.

I went to Safari first and found pay dirt right away in his browsing history. He had been searching for flights on Expedia: SFO to Lihue Airport on Kauai, which I'd been hearing a lot about from Hawaii-vacationing friends. It was supposed to be the nicest of the Hawaiian Islands, though as a native East Coaster, I wouldn't know. I also found a trail of searches on rental car agencies particular to Kauai. This guy wasn't looking at Hertz or Avis—he was checking out the prices on Island Rentals, and from the looks of it, trying to get himself something with real four-wheel muscle. Every listing I saw was a two-door Jeep Wrangler.

This was turning into my kind of manhunt, and Mody was looking more and more like my kind of guy. First the sneakers and now a Jeep. Sure, I preferred something sporty for the city streets, but on an island where you might end up driving on sand? You'd absolutely want four-wheel-drive capability. I would go with a Jeep Wrangler, Rubicon model, with two doors and a hardtop for ease of removal. Not that I spent a lot of time thinking about this sort of thing.

Really. I didn't.

Now all I needed next was a name.

With a bond like his, there was no way Mody could fly out of California using his own credentials. Someone with this much money and a reason to run would have a few other identities at the ready. If he was crooked in one thing, he'd be crooked in many.

I kept poking around. Deep inside the Library folder, I found a special Keychain access with a list of aliases in it. These looked like more than computer names or logins. They looked like real-world identities. The most recent ones used were Doug Harper and Michael MacDonald.

I searched the computer's files for "Doug Harper" and came up with gold: the PDF of a California driver's license in Harper's name but with Mody's picture. I didn't know how he was printing them, but apparently Mody was making his own fake licenses in Photoshop.

Other files in the same folder showed JPEGs of passport pictures taken with Mody's face in a couple of disguises, not good ones. Ultimately, he'd used just his regular picture for the fake passport, which was smart. His fake mustache and wig would have drummed up some notice from any self-respecting TSA agent.

Not that I want to comment on TSA agents and their relative self-respect or lack of it.

I searched for MacDonald's name, as well, and came up with a Canadian passport PDF, again with Mody's picture. This time he had the mustache and a few gold highlights in his dark-brown hair. But as a Canadian, maybe he was just acting the part.

The Harper ID was better work, so I made a mental note to start there when I went looking. I opened his Contacts application to see what he'd last referenced. Sure, most people barely used Contacts on their computers—mostly they just called people from their phones—but I figured it would give me something. And the name it landed on was Mack. Just Mack. Below that was a phone and an email, then "Surf Shack."

That was all I needed, a last nail in the coffin for Kauai. I was ready to hit it.

The next step was the most obvious: get myself to the airport and onto a plane for Kauai. Obvious and essential. Sure, Mody could have faked his searches to make it look like he was flying to Kauai and then didn't, but what fun would that be—for him *or* for me?

If he was *from* Hawaii, had his family there, then he would run there when pressed. Other than the sneakers, it looked as if he had very little in the Bay Area to keep him around. Combine that with a fear of jail and handy fake IDs, and his running almost made sense.

I considered that Leonardi should do a better job of screening his bonds, but that would keep me out of business. Also, the bigger-risk bonds came with a higher premium and a higher payoff. So he kept it up, rolled with the business, and I did the same. All the way to the islands.

4

Call Me Burt

I only packed a few things. What more did I need than a pair of shorts, underwear, and a shirt or two? My toothbrush. I'd buy flip-flops for the beach when I had to, wore a clean pair of size 14 running shoes in case I had to get into anything.

Finding a flight to Kauai on the web wasn't hard, especially with Leonardi footing the bill. I spared him the cost of first class, but sprung for the extra legroom of an exit row. Who knows when they started charging extra for this, but it wasn't a tall person's ideal.

As soon as the receipt came up, I emailed a copy of it to Leonardi, complete with the note: "Bill's on you, buddy. Mody gone to islands under the name Doug Harper. Off to follow."

And just like that I was downstairs, bag in hand, and getting into a stranger's Toyota Prius. Call it a uniquely San Francisco experience, call it techie nirvana, but these new apps got me to the airport with time to spare.

On the seven-and-a-half-hour flight, the dull action movies put me to sleep. As a guy who'd made an action movie, especially one as good as *Shake 'Em Down*, I saw the budgets in Hollywood had shriveled up, the special effects were a lot shakier, and nobody did good stunts anymore. Maybe someday I'd get another crack at it, a chance to make good.

Not long after waking up, I stood outside Lihue Airport. I had not gone to baggage claim, had not declared any fruit or plants. I'd eaten my one mainland-bought apple on the plane, and that was all the fruit Hawaii needed to fear from my visit. I walked right out into the night air and inhaled a huge breath.

Even close to ten o'clock, I smelled summer on the island and felt the heat. A welcome change. I liked not needing a sweater or jacket, and even took off my long-sleeved shirt.

I found the waiting area for rental car shuttles, walked over, and set my bag down to stretch my legs. I held onto a sign post, got into my quads with the one-leg-balance pose. Not that I shied away from yoga, but most of my moves were personal ones I'd invented to loosen up my own self over the years.

Soon the shuttle came for Island Rentals, and I caught it. This was the car place I'd seen in Mody's searches. On our way, I pulled a baseball hat out of my bag and readied my best Midwestern twang.

"Listen here now," I said to the woman at the counter when it was my turn. She stared back through thin, tired eyes. This late, she'd have to be ending her shift soon. I smiled an impossibly friendly smile, holding it until she cracked first, letting down her guard a bit with a smile of her own.

The smile also helped my disguise. Jack Palms, movie actor, never smiled.

She said, "Mahalo. How can I help you?"

I started over. "Sure is a nice night here. Isn't it?"

She nodded.

"Listen, I been following a friend of mine today out to his beach spot. Fellow by the name Doug Harper. Said this was *the* place to get my island Jeep rented, sure enough. You seen him come through today?" I turned to look over the small office, as if some sign of him could be left over. The customers waiting behind me scanned their phones, eager to be distracted from the act of waiting. Nobody recognized me.

Emily—at least this was what her name tag read—glanced around, following my gaze. "Do you see him?"

I turned back, laughing with extra vigor and smiling wide. "I do not, actually. Guess that don't make no sense then because he landed *hours* ago. Likes to get the jump, he does. Know what I mean?" I winked. Maybe I was laying it on too thick, but now I was committed. "I was just wondering, trying to remember, if he said I should get the four-door or the two-door Wrangler?" I acted like this was the most important question of my day. "And if I'm supposed to get the hardtop or the soft?"

Emily tilted her head. "Sir?"

I pointed at her computer. "Don't you have our reservations in there? Doug said made them for both of us last week. Can you look for me?"

"I—?" she started a protest and then gave up. Whether the hour, the bored patrons in line behind me or my bona fide Midwestern appeal got her to look didn't matter. Just that she did. "You said Mr. Harper's reservation?"

"Yes, ma'am. And my name is Anthony Albert Culpepper." I put down a Culpepper driver's license for Tennessee and matching credit card from my wallet. "But you can call me Burt."

Yes, I actually had gone through the trouble of making up a

credit card and driver's license with this alias. On one hand, it had become a hobby to think up just-this-side-of-plausible aliases, ones I could get a kick out of using, and on the other, you tend to benefit from having a lot of fake IDs when your own name carries a level of Hollywood infamy and notoriety to anyone who came of age through the aughts.

"Culpepper," she said. "No, no reservation."

"And not linked at all to my friend Doug Harper?" I waved a finger at her terminal. "Like I mentioned, he *said* he made them for both of us."

She typed and searched, looking over her records. I knew it was a long shot that she would tell me anything about Mody's reservation—Harper's—but crazier things have happened.

"He did check in earlier today. Picked up one car. But no reservation linked to your name, unfortunately."

"Oh, that is unfortunate." I looked outside at the parking lot full of cars, SUVs and certified off-road vehicles. "Those ones out there aren't all spoken for, are they?"

"No, no," she said. "We can get you started."

"Can you see what he rented? I want to get just the same exact thing as him. Okay, miss? You know, I really have no idea what we'll be getting into out here on this island. What with these beaches and all. The sand!"

Emily shot a glance over my shoulder. The length of our session was not going unnoticed by the other vacationers. Only one other counter was open at this time of night, and the agent there was a pimple-faced kid who looked slower than dial-up internet.

"Please just do your best to match us up, ma'am. I'm sure

something went wrong on my reservation." Then, fast as a magician—because this is something I actually practice—I slid a fifty under my driver's license and credit card, and pushed both toward her. "I say, any help you can offer is *greatly* appreciated."

At the sign of the cash she perked up. Tips aren't usually part of renting a car, and this worked to my benefit. "Yes, sir, Mr. Culpepper."

She turned to a board of car keys behind the counter. I saw plenty to choose from on the hooks. As she stepped away from the counter to check what was available, I leaned over to see her computer screen. It still held Doug Harper's reservation, along with a local address on a street name composed mostly of vowels. All I could do was scrawl the letters down on a map she's left on the counter. There was no way I could memorize that strange word.

When Emily turned back, she held up a set of keys. "One two-door Wrangler in silver, just like your friend ordered," she said. "He requested a hardtop. Will that be all right for you?"

I smiled my biggest one yet. "As long as that top do come off, ya hear?"

She told me it did but didn't take that concept any further. I had to be content with my own thoughts on the matter.

As she entered my details into her system, I looked up the strange street address on my phone's navigation app. Luckily, one location on the island popped up, a place my phone could direct me to. As I zoomed out on the screen, I saw that it was on the south side of the island, right near the coast, not more than a half an hour's drive. The street was in an area of resorts and hotels called Poipu.

5

Free Pass

Kauai's main road was a two-lane highway that took me south from the airport along the coast. Once I passed the first gas station and a couple of cheap restaurants, the road wove through lush trees and midnight greenery. Just having the windows open wasn't enough; inspired by the moonlight and the abundance of stars, I pulled off into a scenic viewpoint area and removed the two front sections of the Jeep's hardtop. I stuffed them into the back, and now I had headroom clear up to the stars. Above me and to the right, a series of mountains loomed from the center of the island. Even at night, it was all green and beautiful.

As I started back onto the road, I turned the heat on to keep my feet warm. Best of both worlds.

After a few more gas stations and a small outpost of civilization, the highway turned right and started along the South Shore, parallel to the ocean. Kauai looked every bit like a square on the map, more or less, and I followed along the outside.

Now I could see water, mountains, and stars all around. I felt like I was in a whole new part of the world. Not a city for miles, not anywhere on the island. Nothing like San Francisco, a world far behind me. I was glad Joe had called.

When I hit Poipu my iPhone's navigation started talking a blue streak of vowels, telling me lefts and rights on streets it couldn't come close to pronouncing the right way. Siri's attempts gave me just enough time to recognize signs and choose what to do. Eventually, I came to the address Mody had used to rent his car.

It was a Starbucks in the middle of a small strip mall. Whether or not he knew I was on his tail, this guy was all for fucking with someone. In this case, the someones were Island Rentals and me. One of us had no idea, and one of us didn't like it.

Still, I might have laughed it off and bought myself an iced Frappucino, but the Starbucks was long closed.

That last tidbit from Mody's computer came to mind: the name from his Contacts application, a friend or acquaintance named Mack. I put "Surf Shack" into my phone's navigation. A location close by popped right up: Mack's Poipu Surf Shack. Just a few blocks away, but when I cruised the shop, it was dead closed. Time to call it a night and start again in the morning.

My phone showed me the Poipu Sheraton right on the water, just a few minutes away. I could make do with that, and so could my expense account for Leonardi.

The Sheraton had no bar downstairs, but a busy restaurant on the back side of the building surrounded by torches stuck up on high poles. Whoever came up with the décor, fire was high on his list of favorite aesthetics. Maybe it was there to hypnotize babies and toddlers. From all the families I'd seen at the airport and Island Rentals, Poipu was a very kid-friendly vacation destination.

At close to midnight, the restaurant was open but near-empty. Most everyone in the hotel was tucked into bed. I sat at the bar and ordered a club soda.

The barkeep asked how I was, then looked at me twice, a quick second glance like he knew me but wasn't sure from where. He didn't place me from the movie, which was good. The less of that the better, as far as I was concerned.

"Better order fast," he said. "Kitchen's going to close."

"What's good?" I looked over the menu.

He waved a hand at the windows just a few tables away. "There's the ocean. Right there. Pick anything in it. The boys'll cook it up. Best seafood around."

I turned around and sure enough there was the Pacific, big and dark beyond the torches.

I told him I'd take a burger.

"Good choice. All our beef is locally raised on the island. Pasture style. Best meat you can eat in the United States."

I went out of my way to seem interested and grateful. Any info from a local about Mack's Surf Rental was worth being nice for.

When I was ready to get down to it, I said, "Buddy of mine back on the mainland said I can get whatever I need from Mack's Surf Shack. That so?"

"Mack's got the goods. Snorkels, surfboards, whatever. You name it."

He knew the Surf Shack well because Mack came in every

now and then to bend his ear, watch the waves, and scout tourists. He'd recognize someone he'd rented to, and they'd buy him a drink or vice versa, and then he'd talk to people at other tables and offer them special deals if they came into his shop.

"Mack's a staple of the local economy." Then the barkeep leaned over the bar, raised his eyebrows. "Bud, you got no ring on your finger and don't strike me as the type to have kids. What are you really here looking for?"

I didn't crack wise about Mack or tell him I was after Mody, just waited to see what he'd offer. When he said nothing, I answered, "Whatever's here. I'm just happy to be on the island."

He smiled, went back to wiping glasses. "Clean living, man. Plenty of that all around."

I waited, but he didn't say anything else.

Soon, a pretty waitress brought my burger out on an open-faced bun next to a side of fries. It all looked good. Her included. She had short, straight, dark hair and a wicked smile, plus long legs sticking out of short, black shorts—the kind of legs I wanted to wrap around me. When she winked at me after setting it down, I started getting into the island vibe.

The barkeep nodded in the waitress's wake. I guess he could tell I wasn't just eyeing the burger.

I slid the plate closer and ate.

After the burger, my waitress came back and gave me my bill. She told the barman it was time for her to cash out and she'd have his tips in a few minutes.

"Have a drink with me?" I asked.

She ordered a martini, then took off her apron and said she'd be right back. I met the bartender's dark eyes as she left. He smiled, but not like he was rooting for me. When he had finished making her drink, he set it on a napkin and then went down to the other end of the bar. She came back in a bit and took the stool next to me. I had my room key down on my bill, just in case she wondered.

Her uniform was all black: little shorts and a tight tee. I might have been checking out her legs a little too much because she said, "You staying here long?" as if to get my attention back up to her face.

"I might be."

"And you always buy the girls drinks?"

"Anything you want." I held her eye contact, not backing down. I was ready to pony up, whether her order was on the menu or off.

She just stared right back, not laughing, and finally smiled. I could see her teeth. She stuck her hand out and we shook. Formal-like.

"Gina," she said.

"Jack."

"Big movie stars don't often happen in here. Not on my shift, anyway."

"Call me lucky."

The bartender had made her drink clear to the brim, so she had to go down over it like a hummingbird over a blossom. Two olives bumped gently at its base.

Suddenly the bartender was back to break my groove. He snapped his fingers. "*That's* where I recognize you from. That movie. What was it called?"

Gina turned to me and said, "Been a while, though. Hasn't it, Jack?"

The barkeep raised his eyebrows at me, still waiting for his answer.

I said, "Nothing new in a few years, but you know what they say about actors? We're always as good as our next part."

"You got one?"

"No. Not a chance."

They both laughed, part with me and part at my expense. I could take it.

Gina said, "Don't you mean as good as your last part?"

"That too." I nodded. "However long ago that was."

"*Shake 'Em Down*," she said. "That was my brother's favorite movie when I was in tenth grade."

I did the mental math. I wasn't aged out of the ballgame.

The bartender wiped his hands on a towel and said, "Yeah. I remember that one. Pretty good, too." He smiled, and I could guess he'd be about the same age as her brother. Right in my target demographic back then. He shook my hand, said it was nice to meet me, and acted like he didn't want to take the selfie we both knew he wanted. I asked for his phone and leaned in to take it for him. When he had that, he rushed off to share it on his networks. That gave us some space.

"So what *is* the next project?" Gina asked.

"I'll let you know when I get it."

"That's not what you're doing here?"

I tapped the rim of my club soda. "You could say I'm here on a location scout."

She nodded with a look that agreed to a certain level of Hollywood BS, as if no one in the movie industry was to be entirely trusted.

"What else you got going?" she asked.

"I'm keeping it together."

Now she properly raised her martini and offered me a toast. We touched glasses. "To keeping it together," she said.

She appraised me physically, looking me over up and down, and not like she was sizing me up for the chopping block, either. More like she was considering the whole buy. She didn't look away, held my eye contact just a little too long, as if to tell me she was open to whatever I might say. When I didn't say anything, she smiled.

"Where you from?" I asked.

She told me she landed in Hawaii a few months back, after she plain gave up on the winters in Minneapolis. Kauai was as good an answer as any other—until she arrived and found the locals discriminated against outsiders who wanted to make their visits permanent.

"Try finding an apartment here or getting a job." She waved at the bar. "Unless you're working for a big corporation like Sheraton, you're all but shut out."

The bartender walked down the bar, wiping a glass. If I had to guess, he was a local.

"So where you live?"

"I found a place. It's okay. Sharing with another mainlander who bought here. She needed someone to stay in her in-law, keep an eye on the house when she's not around, which is most of the time. She also has a place in LA." Gina fingered her glass's stem, then brought the martini up and took a long drink. Two olives bumped down the side as she did, and she snatched one of them with her teeth. When she finished chewing, she said, "Mostly it's all mine. So that's nice."

I wanted to say something about heading there, asking if she was ready to ditch this bar. I touched my glass: nothing but ice. I wanted to come right out and say something, but that never went well for me sober. Curse of an addict, in some ways: I tried to stay away from booze or anything that could cloud my thinking, and sometimes I was so successful it hurt me.

Here, sober as a stone, anything I imagined saying sounded lecherous or dumb.

She turned to me then with a new look in her eye, like she was half-desperate and about to try something crazy. "You know what a free pass list is?"

I shook my head.

"Let's say you're with a guy, like I was back in the Twin Cities. We dated on and off for about three years. Maybe he's part of why I came out here." She waved her hand. "Anyway, doesn't matter. One night we made a free pass list of famous people we could each sleep with if ever given the opportunity."

I tried not to laugh or smile, but wanted to do both. Things could be turning my way.

"Basically it was something that was unlikely to ever happen."

"And I was on yours?" I smiled despite myself.

Now she laughed. "No. That'd be too corny and coincidental. Wouldn't it?"

I shifted my weight on my chair.

"But when I was younger… maybe. Your movie was cool, funny, *something*. Let's just say that you were considered." She didn't laugh as she said it, then looked me over hard and finished her drink.

"You took Brad Pitt instead?"

"Basically," she said. "But now look who's here in the flesh." She winked.

I smiled. "Bird in the hand?"

"This might sound corny, but what do you say, cowboy? You want to get out of here?"

"I do. You've known that since you sat down."

She put her hand over mine, faster than I expected. Quick hands, this one.

She leaned closer, and I could feel her breath. "I'm not easy, Jack. You still have to treat me right. That means no kinky shit, no rough stuff, nothing wild that I don't like or ask for, and you act the gentleman unless I specifically tell you not to." She paused, making sure her words sunk in. They had. "Got it?"

I nodded. "Yes, ma'am."

"A girl has to protect herself. Nothing on the internet from either of us."

"Definitely not."

She smiled. "Guess you learned that lesson."

My hand on my chest, I said, "You can't get safer than being with me, my lady."

Maybe her lip trembled, either with a laugh or something deeper. Likely it was the drink. I stepped out of my chair and took her hand to help her out of hers. My room key still on the bar, I signed the tab fast and followed her out.

Soon enough, we'd be upstairs peeling back the bedspread, and a whole lot more.

6

Take It Easy

I was the first to wake, so it was my play. I considered what Gina had said the night before. I didn't want to do wrong by her, but it hadn't sounded like she was eager for anything long-term, and I wasn't planning on sticking around after my work for Leonardi was done. So I made what was probably a mistake and got up and out before she woke. The best reason I can offer was that I figured on it being the gentlemanly thing to do.

Not the right choice, I would come to realize. Take care of the woman first: that's what I should have learned long ago.

Instead, I went downstairs, got a coffee and found a chair by the pool.

Eager vacationers ran by, starting their days with a jog along the beach. A year ago I'd have forced myself to do the same, trying to earn back some karmic points for all my fuckups in LA. Now I let the sun warm me, allowing a few simple pleasures like coffee, the topless Jeep, sex without attachments, and the possibility of a swim in the ocean later. All free of guilt, more or less.

I was still on mainland time so I had an hour to kill before Mack's Shack opened.

After my coffee, I made do with a walk along the beach, on the hard part of the sand, toeing the cold water as the waves rolled in. Through meditation and mantras, I had convinced myself that such things were even better than a cigarette. Now I was doing my best to make it true.

Poipu looked to be mainly a family spot, more kids with shovels and pails than a beach full of bikini girls, but I did see a turtle poke its head out of the surf. A big one.

Just take it easy, I told myself. *Enjoy it.*

I headed next to Mack's Surf Shack to see what he would give up about Mody. As soon as I walked in, the proprietor greeted me himself.

"Jack Palms!" He stuck his hand in my direction, then grabbed mine and pumped it when I didn't react fast enough. "What you doing on island, man?"

I hoped no tourists were around to hear him. He wore a smile as wide as Texas and twice as warm.

"Here I am," I said, "right at the end of your arm. I can hear you all the way over here."

He didn't get me, kept talking as if we were outside in a wind tunnel. "What can I do you for, Jack?"

"Looking for the best surf spot on Kauai."

"Yeah, brother. Nice!" Mack winked and pulled me toward the back of the store. "I got the good stuff back here for you, my man." He stopped, regarded me for a moment or several. "If you're up for a publicity pic, that is."

Always an angle.

The shop's back wall was lined with signed photos of him with celebrities. There he was, posing and mugging with the likes of Sly Stallone, Pierce Brosnan, Whoopi Goldberg, and Beau Bridges.

He pointed at the center photo. "You know Pierce has a house on island, right? Owns a bar up in Hanalei, too."

"Pierce?" I asked.

He nodded. "Hanilei Bay? North shore. Good surf up there at Tunnels if you're going."

"Tunnels?" Inside his glass counter I saw a collection of odd items: everything from snorkels and scuba masks to water pipes and diving knives.

"Listen, Mack. I'd be happy to take a picture with you so long as you keep it quiet that I'm here. Publicity and all, you know?"

"Definitely, man. *Def*initely. I get you." He winked, then came around the counter to stand next to me. He held out his cell phone for a selfie of us both, and I smiled my best Hollywood bright.

"That's my man. I'll get that printed up today, and you can sign it when you return your equipment." He slipped the phone into a back pocket of his shorts. "So what are you renting, then? Surfboard? Snorkel?"

When I pointed outside at the Jeep, he smiled. "Tell me where I can get that thing on some sand. It's rented, and I'm not getting my money's worth unless I can beat it up some."

"Oh, I hear you. Absolutely. And I know just the beach." He showed me some local spots on a map, the roads to get to them and where to get onto the sand.

"That's not all I need, though." I stepped back, ready to get serious. "I'm looking for a friend of yours. Name of Mody. He said to call if I ever made the island."

"Which Mody?"

I stopped for a second, wondering what my options were. "Meyer," I said.

"M&Ms is here?" He shook his head. "No, way. I doubt that."

I waited him out.

He said, "Far as I know, Eminem hasn't been on island in a year or more. He's in Frisco, man. San Fran."

Even as a non-native of San Francisco, this duo of nicknames hit my ears like fingernails on a blackboard.

"What about Doug Harper? You know him?"

"The baseball player?"

"No. I don't think so."

Mack wrinkled his nose. "Then no. Never heard of him."

I nodded, trying to sniff out what else he knew. "If Mody was on the island, any idea where I could find him?"

He shook his head, uber-expressive now, really looking like he had no idea.

"He's your old buddy, right? No idea where he might hang out?"

He squinted his eyebrows together and said, "Not very island to be wondering so much, huh, Jack? What's the real deal here?" He held up a finger and gave it just the hint of a wave.

I tried to ignore it. "I heard that he blew out of SF with some troubles tailing and made it back here. Let's say a friend of ours wants to know."

I winked. On one hand, I wanted to sound apologetic,

friendly-like, but really I was considering two options: the first was to go violent, try to beat some info out of the old surfer, and the second was to politely leave, then watch his shop and try to see if he made any phone calls.

"Let me get you a surfboard or a snorkel. You should definitely see fish, at least, while you're here." Mack went around the desk. "Have you surfed before? I mean, of course Jack Palms has surfed, but like, what style of board you feeling?"

I decided the second method sounded better. Violence as a last resort. Especially in the land of resorts.

I told Mack I'd take some snorkel gear and try looking at the fish near my hotel. He got happy about that, told me I was getting the "local's discount." We put together a couple of items, enough to fill my arms, and he shuffled me toward the door.

I tossed the rented stuff in the back of my Jeep, turned to Mack, and got caught in a four-part handshake I wasn't prepared for. He said he promised to have that photo printed and blown up for me to sign by that afternoon.

I got into the Jeep, started her up, and pulled out of the lot. When I was about a hundred yards up the road, just past the first turn, I parked off to the side amid the greenery. Then I jumped out and walked back to the shop.

7

Tune Up

I could hear Mack on the phone when I crept around the side of his shack. He was laughing and talking trash; BS-ing like he was on with an old friend. I stayed down below the window line, working over to a door in the rear.

"Glad to have you back, boy. Mahalo."

If Mody wasn't on the other end, I'd eat that phone. Mack got off with a promise to see somebody soon.

I walked in the back door and came up to stand behind the counter. "My man Mack," I said.

He spun around fast. "Shit, Jack. What the—?"

I stepped around the counter, closing our distance by half. "What are we doing about Meyer Mody today? You were just talking to him, right?"

"This ain't no movie, Jack."

"Sure enough," I said. "Now show me."

He came right at me, telegraphing and looping into a long swing, a really wide, high haymaker that didn't have a chance. I was about a foot ahead of it, stepped left and watched him sail by, then delivered a hard right just between his gut and his solar plexus. Right away I knew that was enough. It knocked the air out of him in a huff, and he slumped back against a wall. Two snorkel masks fell off their display hooks.

"Oh, man. I can't breathe."

I watched him, waiting it out.

He wheezed. "Jack!"

"Just give yourself a minute, man. You'll be okay."

Soon the whistling in his chest stopped. His face was no longer red.

I crouched down in front of him so our eyes met. "Now," I said, "let's talk."

I pushed a chair around the counter, rolled it over to him. He crawled up onto it and then slumped back, looking like some critical piece of his metal had melted. He produced a pack of cigarettes from the cargo pocket of his shorts and asked me to pass him a lighter off the floor. I did and he nodded. Once he'd lit up his smoke, the color started creeping back into his face.

I'd been doing my level best to lay off the smokes and mainly winning that battle, but to see him smoking right then, it tugged at my desires. Call it nerves or adrenaline, something from the beast was running through me. I'd been doing well for a long time.

My heart was beating wild drums. I said, "Those'll kill you," and reached for the pack.

He nodded, and I took one and lit up. The first drag brought in a wave of nausea that calmed me way down. Nerves and all, everything went right to dull. Good.

"So what you say, Mack. You want to tell me a story?"

"Why the fuck not?" He picked a bit of tobacco off his lip and studied it. "But what you gonna do? Soon as I tell you where he is, and you leave to get him, I make a call and he gone. How that help you?"

I just stared at him, wished more strength into my legs. I didn't need the smoking habit or anything else to remind me of the old times. Every day of my current situation, every day I wasn't on a set making serious bank, was reminder enough.

I ground out the cigarette against his glass countertop and stepped toward my man.

He put his hands up. "Okay. Say you hurt me. You really want to go and do that to find Mody? What did he do to you?" He pushed himself up and took two steps away.

Mack was good-sized, but he looked like a man who'd been beaten: a stinger under the ribcage will do that. Knock a guy's wind out, he doesn't want it knocked out again.

He sucked in his chest and gathered himself, though, as if he wanted to do something a tough guy might. After taking a last drag, he flicked his cigarette out the front door into the gravel parking lot.

He looked right at me, standing up almost to my height. "Come on, Jack. What you really going to do here?"

I faked a jab at his face to get his guard up, then hit him once in the gut, doubling him up and knocking him down to size. "You lied to me, Mack. What am I gonna do? I'm gonna work you over."

I hit him again in the liver, this time holding his shoulder with my left hand to keep him in position.

I said, "Do I have a choice?"

He groaned and dribbled spit onto the floor, barely missing his flip-flops.

"Hurts, huh? You have a choice, Mack."

I pushed him back hard against the wall. More masks and goggles and swim fins fell to the ground. He fell into his chair, tilted his head back, sucking wind. I could have hit him hard in the neck, really fucked up his Adam's apple, but I refrained.

"Listen, man. This sucks for us both." I had to laugh. "Well, more for you than for me. But I have to know when you're telling the truth. So here's an incentive."

I hit him again in the solar plexus. He gasped, wheezing. His face came down to his knees, and I wasn't sure if he would throw up. His eyes were closed. I watched him, counted out loud to twenty.

Once he had his breath, he kept coughing.

"You with me now? Ready to make the right choice."

He held his hand up, like to tell me to wait a minute.

"No bullshit, Mack. Now or we do some more work."

"Fuck, Jack. Fuck." I could barely hear him, but he was nodding. He sat up the best he could, ready to cooperate.

"Maybe we go for a ride now, find him together. What do you say to that?"

He stood up. It was the right move.

I walked him outside and watched him lock up the surf shop. Then we marched back to my Jeep. He moved slowly, stopping twice to rest with his hands on his knees, spitting onto the gravel and dirt along the roadside. I had half an idea to get the Jeep and come back for him, but didn't. Walking it off would do him some good.

By the time we made it to the car, he was mostly upright. I helped him climb in and he slumped way down in his seat. When

I reached around to buckle his seat belt, he barely moved. "Breathe, motherfucker," I told him. "Keep breathing."

Then I went around to the driver's side and climbed in.

"Where to?" I asked.

He pointed for me to turn around and head back toward the water. At the first rotary, he directed me west, back out onto the main road, following a path along the southern coast.

He waved, trying to get my attention, so I leaned in close to hear. "Going to the end of the line," he said, his voice hoarse. "Mody got a place out by that locals-only beach I told you about."

"He better." I looked at Mack sideways, keeping up the tough act.

"It's a long drive. Why don't we get a drink. Let me buy you a mai tai. Some water."

"It's not even eleven."

"Water?"

I drove without answering. Two small towns and ten minutes later, he was almost sitting up straight. In a louder voice, he said, "Not to typecast you, but you play the good guy much better."

"I can play the good guy here. Just don't give me any more bullshit."

Mack held his hands up. "I hear you, Jack. Listen, I ain't no fighter. Neither is M&Ms. We work this out like pals, okay?"

I said, "You take me to him, we're good. You fuck with me or we go someplace else, I'm gonna give you more body work—a full engine overhaul. Then you'll know what we did before was just a tune up. That okay?" I asked. "Tell me you think it's fine. Tell me you hear me."

He did.

8

Oceanfront Property

We drove west another five miles or so on 50, out through towns called Kalaheo, Eleele and Hanapepe.

Everything on the island looked to be close on a map, but when you tried to get from one point to another, it took time. The towns were small, not big enough to warrant attention and not near enough to be called close. Both sides of the road were lined with waist-high green bushes. Beyond them, always to my left, I could intermittently see the ocean. Above us to the right, a mountain loomed.

Mack kept quiet, which I liked, but after a while I got curious.

"Let me ask you," I said, "what kind of name is Meyer Mody?"

He shook his head. "His family Indian or something. Maybe the only ones on island."

"And what's up with your man's collection of sneakers? He a freak about those, or what?"

As soon as I mentioned the sneakers, Mack perked up. Something lit a fire in him, and he turned to me, the frog gone from his throat and a fresh twinkle in his eye.

"His kicks? Shit, that boy crazy for sneakers. We both were.

And that ain't normal on the island. But he *still* is. Freaking fanatic. That's my man, though. A fiend since way back."

I kept my eyes on the road. "Looked like he left his whole collection back in California. I saw it at his house. Some *nice* ones."

"No way," he said. "That can't be his whole collection. Probably just his flips. The ones he cop and then put right on eBay." He waved it off like I had no idea.

"On eBay? Who buys them?"

"The fuck knows? Kids in Japan? Rich dudes in NYC or Russia? *Something*. Motherfuckers *pay*, though."

I filed it away. I had more questions but didn't know where to start.

Mack was loosening up. "I never even knew about kicks before Mody. My boy ahead of the game. Started selling way back before eBay. He always been a collector."

"Does he wear the kicks, too? I see you don't."

I still had my city sneakers on, just a pair of Air Max I'd picked up at Niketown in Union Square, but he didn't seem to have noticed or cared. If I were smart, I'd have grabbed a pair of flip-flops from his shop while we were still there. Let my toes enjoy the sun.

Mack laughed. "Shit, on island, it always just slippers. All anybody wears. *If that*. Least during the day. Back in when we was kids, Mody have all his J's sent over from the mainland. Used to break 'em out in high school and girls be following him down the halls."

"J's?"

"Jordans, man. *Jordans*."

Even I had to let that sit for a few breaths, out of respect.

"You know who sent them?"

"He had an aunt or somebody in Oakland. Something like that." He held a hand up. "All I know."

I'd seen each of the Jordan releases on kids around me when I was growing up, knew people in LA with closets full of them, but had never owned a pair. What can I say? I never thought they were my style. But holding the Air Jordan XI in Mody's house— those fabled Elevens—changed something inside me. It was like now that I'd held them, I knew they were attainable. As an adult, I could afford them, so now I wanted my own. But I had no idea where to start or how to find my size.

We passed a series of palm trees on the left. The road wound closer to the water so that beaches were right alongside us. Then it turned to dirt. I considered putting on the four-wheel drive, I *wanted to,* but the road didn't call for it. Not yet.

"Mody's place way back here off this road," Mack said. "Out on sand only. You'll need to get real with this Jeep. Give you just what you wanted."

"Yeah?"

"He bought out here to keep away from tourists. Shit, you should see where I live. I can't buy like Mody, not with the way real estate going. Vacationers buying up all the Kauai they can get."

"Even out here?" I gestured to the road: what few houses I could see were set way back from the beach. They didn't look big enough or new enough for a mainlander to want. Plus, we were well over an hour from the airport.

"Shit yes. All of this. Mody been trying to buy up places like investments. Acting all the productive capitalist. But he strapped as shit now, *he says*, owes that bank and the Koloas some *serious* money."

"Like how much?" I thought about Mody's crime, wondering what had brought him all the way back here. "What are the Koloas?"

"Bad dudes," he said.

We got to the end of the dirt road. All that stretched in front of us was sand. I stopped the car, letting it idle.

"I hear you're supposed to lock the wheel differentials," I said. "You know anything about that?"

"Fuck, man. This a rental? What's a differential?"

I checked the tires that I could see below me. "We're supposed to lower the tire pressure for driving on sand."

"Sound like a reference manual." He pointed through the windshield at the sand. "Where your spirit of adventure, Jack?" He laughed, and I got the sense that Mody, or any local, wouldn't have stopped for a moment before driving out onto the beach.

I thought about the Jeep, the sand, the standing of the credit card in the name of one Albert Anthony Culpepper, and I said, "Fuck it." I shifted to neutral and switched down to four-wheel drive. Then I shifted back into drive and gunned us out onto the beach.

As soon as we hit the sand, the car lurched, paused for a moment, and I pumped the gas. When the wheels caught, we shot out toward the water.

Mack's body popped out of his seat against the seat belt, and he swore.

I wrestled the steering wheel right and then straight again as the tires found their way into the ruts already left in the sand. It felt good. We picked up speed and the driving took more wrestling, more work, but I could feel the wind off the ocean and from our speed, and it was fun.

Mack reached for the radio and turned it on, then up. An island radio station crooned out a love song for the beach, blasting from our speakers. Leonardi's face flashed through my mind, and I felt a little bit bad about having a good time while I was supposed to be working.

I turned the music down. "We're heading to Mody, right?"

"Yeah, man. You know it." He pointed to my left, out into the water. "See those tubes? I should be surfing."

I saw a couple of surfers carving up the waves on short boards. One paddled into a swell, got up fast and rode along the tunnel created by the whitewater.

The car lurched again, popping me out of my seat against the belt. I steered into the ruts, following where other tires had been. After a few minutes, houses started to appear on our right behind the trees. First just one, then eventually a few more.

"His up here," Mack said. He pointed at a stand of three houses. "Last one. The gray."

The last house was on the other side of a sand berm, tucked back under a big, weeping tree. The structure looked low and dark, but I saw a rental Jeep nearly identical to mine parked under the front overhang.

I angled out of the ruts and up the sand. We bounced like a

boat in waves, and I liked it. I could have slowed, but where was the fun in that?

Toward the top of the beach the sand got harder, more packed, and something like a driveway led to the house.

Mack hooted. "M&Ms! Got some visitors!"

I backhanded him in the chest, knocking him against his seat.

His words cut off in a croak, but it was too late: I saw a curtain ruffle in an upstairs window as I put the Jeep into park and pulled the brake.

9

Jeeps on the Beach

As soon as the Jeep came to a full stop, I was out the door and onto the dirt, headed for the steps. Now was the time to have a gun, and I didn't. Just another lack of firepower in a long and suspect lack of weaponry in my life.

"Stay there," I yelled back to Mack. I took the stairs two at a time up to the second floor deck space and flung open the screen door to the house.

Instead of knocking on the wooden door, I tried the handle. It opened. I poked my head inside and pulled it back. Nothing. No movement, no shots fired, no sounds. All I had seen inside was an empty living room.

"Mody, we need to talk!"

I listened for a few beats and heard nothing. Then I stepped into the living room.

I saw a TV and couch to my left, a full kitchen directly ahead.

"Mody?"

Nothing.

"M&Ms? Where you at, Mody? Come on out so we can talk. Let's make this easy."

I stepped farther into the house and saw a short hallway to

my right that ended in a closed door. I followed it past a bathroom and a small bedroom and opened the door. A quick look inside showed another empty bedroom. I went in and saw a double-folding-door closet. I opened that and found a handful of pristine Nike running sneakers lining the shelves. This was Mody's place, all right. But it looked like nobody had been living here for a long while.

In the back of the closet was a wooden ladder.

I looked up. What would be the pros and cons of climbing up into a crawl space or storage area? I chose not to. Even if Mody was up there, I was staying all Bartleby on this.

On the other side of the bed was a big bay window. I could see palm trees outside, and as I got closer, the twin Jeeps downstairs. Mack still sat in the passenger seat of mine. I knocked on the glass and pointed two fingers at my eyes and then at him.

He smiled and gave me the finger.

Behind me, I heard movement from the living room.

"Mody!" I turned and rushed back down the hall into the house's great room. Something crashed at the opposite end of the house, beyond the kitchen.

"Hey!"

I rushed into the kitchen area and saw another hallway to my right. This one led to the master bedroom, and its door was wide open.

"Come on, Mody. Let's talk."

I heard a crash and then a Jeep motor starting outside.

"The *fuck*?" I rushed into the bedroom and saw a small dog, a Terrier, tied to a chest of drawers. Next to the chest was a

47

broken lamp on the floor. The dog yipped at me and pulled at its leash.

"Motherfucker."

I ran to the window in time to see Mack standing up in the passenger seat of Mody's Jeep as Mody backed it out.

Mack yelled, "Suck it, *actor!*" loud enough for me to hear through the glass.

There was Mody, right down there in the driveway, gunning his Jeep backward onto and over the berm toward the sand.

I ran back through the living room and out onto the porch, swearing a blue streak. By the time I got to the stairs, I could see the bastards had punctured my tires. It was already listing to one side. I caught just their Jeep's taillights and frame bumping over the top of the berm to the sand.

I rushed to my Jeep and hopped in. Maybe the thing would drive on sand with *really* low tire pressure. Or no air. I could hope. Plus, maybe I had a minute or two before the air really leaked out.

I hoped for the best as I slammed home the keys, started the engine, and pushed the wheel hard to the right to get after them in drive. A few of Mody's beach chairs in the driveway got under my tires, but I wasn't sweating them either—I heard just a double crunch as they passed underneath.

Mody's roll bar was just visible on the beach as I came around.

As I drove forward, the Jeep straightened out into a wicked lean. They'd punctured the tires on just my side, enough to slow me down considerably and keep the car from any long-distance chases, but not enough to keep me off the sand, even if I was leaning. Maybe I could catch them before the thing got stuck.

The lower-pressure wheels caught as I hit the sand. I gunned it and the tires on the other side spun. I shot forward and hard to the right, then cranked the steering wheel and gunned it again. Finally all the tires caught, more or less, and carried me ahead at an angle—unless I kept fighting the wheel. I struggled back to straight and tried to follow in Mody's fresh tracks.

They were still less than twenty yards ahead of me. Blame the sand and slow going; blame them not thinking I'd even get out. Mack pointed back at me, laughing. I kept on swearing.

The Jeep handled terribly, but by wrestling the wheel with both hands, I was able to keep it straight while the tires lost air. Mody began zig-zagging up and down the beach to spread his tracks, but I kept on straight, a boat against the current, crashing over the lumps of his wake, pushing the Jeep to go as fast as it could. I might have reached almost twenty-five miles per.

I was making up ground. Mack tapped Mody on the shoulder, and I could see him say something like, "He's gaining."

Then, as Mody turned from the land side of the beach, he headed straight into my path and slammed on the brakes. I cranked the wheel to avoid the collision, but the Jeep barely changed its direction; my right front end smacked hard into his back left. The steering wheel hit my chest, but not enough to slow me down; wearing no seat belt let me get out faster. I was out onto the sand and standing on Mody's running board a moment before he could accelerate away.

Then he popped forward and all I could do was hang on to keep myself upright.

Mody turned toward the ocean, picking up speed on the

hard-packed wet sand. My foot slipped, and Mack tried to shove me off. Instead, I kneed him in the side of his head, holding the roll bar for leverage. The car swerved again, and I was almost thrown.

Mody had his hands full controlling the wheel. I got my feet under me, then looked up.

That's when I saw the gun.

Mody had a nickel-plated .45 aimed at me from the driver's seat. He said, "Let go, asshole. Step off."

"You wouldn't."

But I froze for that moment as I looked down the gun's barrel, and in that next second Mack pushed me away, shoved me off the running board. I landed on the sand.

Their Jeep turned back up the beach toward the island's center, away from the water, and they cruised away with Mack smiling like a mad hatter.

I kicked sand in disgust, stranded, and trudged the thirty yards back to my own lame Jeep, which was sinking lower and lower on its two flat tires.

10

A Woman Scorned

I'd hiked back to the highway before I saw a single car. When I did, the driver was an old surfer who was happy to pick me up and talk my ear off. He dropped me at the nearest gas station, where I convinced a grease-stained Samoan to take me back out to the beach in his tow truck.

Call the afternoon wasted, then, along with three hundred bucks on new tires for the Jeep. I had no idea how Island Rentals would react to that or the big dent in the front bumper. Leonardi's problem, I decided.

Back at my hotel, I went up to my room and flopped onto the bed. I wanted a beer and a cigarette, but instead I lay on the mattress and watched the ceiling fan spin, trying to figure out my next move.

That's when I heard a pounding on the door.

"The fuck, Jack?" It was Gina. I hadn't been careful about coming in through the lobby, didn't even think to sneak by. As a grown man, more or less, I would take responsibility for myself.

"Open the fucking door, asshole."

Taking grown-man responsibility was about to get tougher.

I looked around the room: at least she hadn't ransacked the

51

place. What few items I'd brought with me were still there.

She pounded on the door. "I know you're in there."

I pushed back up to my feet, sighed, and straightened up. I didn't hurry. When I opened the door, she took one step into the room, turned to face me, and slapped my right cheek.

I said, "I might've deserved that."

She stood there a moment and then tried to knee me in the balls. I saw it coming in and blocked it. "*That* I don't deserve."

She glowered. I didn't think she'd been crying, but her energy was all over the place, something radiating off her like a knocked down power line.

"You," she said.

"Now, come on. Let's talk about this."

She punched me in the chest, closed-fisted. A good shot. I admired that in her. I coughed. Hoping to calm her down, I reached out for her shoulders. Another mistake. She kneed me again and got my thigh this time. I took a couple of steps back. The door closed on its own.

"You think I'm some kind of fun-time toy for you? Is that it, Jack?"

"I thought I was doing you a favor."

"Asshole. You think you're some kind of gift to a woman just because you acted in one crappy movie?"

"Sorry. No, that's not what I—"

"The fuck it isn't. Fuck *you*!"

I stood there and let that roll by.

Her shoulders worked up and down. She pushed her bangs away from her face. "That's not me, Jack."

"No. I mean, I thought we said we were just—"

"No. I don't do this. That's not me. You don't leave." She tried another swing. I backed away again. This time I kept my hands up.

"Come on," I said. "I'm sorry about that. I made a mistake. Okay?"

That took some of the wind out of her sails. She sat down on the bed, exhaled hard. "Then make it right, Jack."

"What do you mean?"

"Don't leave."

I did a double-take, something like out of *Scooby-Doo*. "What? I'm just here on work."

"Stay here."

"I can't. I don't—"

"Right. But I'm not here for long, either. This place doesn't fit me."

"Okay," I said. "Tell me what I can do."

"I need you to help me get some money a guy owes me."

"I— What?" I should have seen this heading directly at me like an eighteen-wheeler bearing down on a rabbit. But I hadn't. I didn't. Instead I stayed right in its path. And kept on there.

She said, "It won't take long."

I let out a sigh. Not only was the truck bearing down, but I was choosing to stay in its way.

"Tell me who he is. And where." I knew I'd be flying back to San Francisco in a couple of days, or less, and that Gina would be passing out of my life and I out of hers. But in that moment I wanted to help her. Maybe I'm just a romantic. Or an idiot. In that moment, though, I agreed.

"He's a guy I used to work for. Up on the north shore in

Hanalei Bay. Just a bar. I quit, and he never paid me."

"So why can't you just go back?"

She shrugged. "Maybe I don't have a car. Maybe I never want to see that place or the people in it again." She had a look on her face like something bad had happened there.

I felt like it might make me a real gentleman if I went up there and made things right, or just brought back her money. Maybe it would. In any case, I said I'd make things right for her. I think I meant it, too. Call it some kind of karmic balancing act: I had fucked up that morning, should've known it or seen the reminder when people were all out jogging and I was sitting on my ass. Now I was getting the kickback from it and a chance to make something right.

That was how I found myself in the Jeep a half-hour later, heading toward the far side of the island, to the North Shore and a bar called Bar Acuda. On the map it didn't look to be far, but from what I was learning about the island, distances were deceiving.

I wasn't anybody's bagman, not a bill collector or an enforcer, but I was off on her errand, putting my own life on hold to drive to the other coast.

I told myself there were worse things, worse places I could be than on Kauai in a two-door Jeep with the top off, driving these roads, but maybe I had no idea then what I was really getting into. Or maybe I was doing the right thing all along.

11

Bar Acuda

I had to loop all the way back to the island's east side and then up along the whole eastern coast, past the airport and through Kapaa, then halfway around the North Shore to get to Hanlei Bay. Kauai only has one highway, and it wraps around the island's perimeter on three sides—all but the western, the Na Pali Coast, which is inaccessible to everything but hikers and helicopters.

I considered Mody and Leonardi, but that trail was stone cold. Anything else I could find would be more work, likely back on the computer or just out sniffing the air for the aroma of Jordans. The least I could do was to call Leonardi and check in.

He answered right away. "Better have something good for me, Jack. Don't waste my time. Or my money."

"Me? Never."

"You're in paradise, ain't you? Where the shit you think I am?"

I almost said something about the fog—*almost*—but knew he wouldn't want to hear that. I just grunted in the affirmative.

"Well, I'm in SF for starters. Someplace where the weather isn't what you've got there. I'm sitting in my fucking office. So do like the song says and tell me something good."

I offered the best news I could think of: that I knew a way he could recoup *some* of his money by getting out to Tiburon and carting off Mody's collection of sneakers.

"The fuck I'm gonna do with that?" he asked. "Did I look like fucking eBay the last time you saw me? Am I the freaking internet?"

"Sorry. Thought that might help."

"Fuck. Give me something better."

I said, "I'm getting close here. Following up on a few good leads and making real progress."

"You find our guy?"

"Not quite yet."

He made a sound like that statement was the bullshit that it was, and said, "You have two days. Get him. Get back. Get my money. Hear?"

I did hear.

The tricky and sometimes ugly part of the job was this: the people whose money I was after, and also spending, did not like to lose it—*any of it*. And if I lost them money, they'd make it my problem, my money. So if I didn't come back with Mody, Leonardi was going to take it out of my ass.

I said, "I hear you, Joe." But he had already hung up.

By the time I got up to the North Shore, it was already eight o'clock.

Hanalei looked like a smoked-out little surfing town, which it was. The place had all the swagger of a stoned surfer crossing the two-lane street at his own pace. That and a grocery store with a big parking lot.

I parked in front of a place that sold shaved ice and got out to look around for the bar. Turned out it was right across the street from me. Easy to find. The name Bar Acuda made it seem smart, but not too smart.

When I walked in, I could tell the place was trying to put the stoned surfer vibe far behind it. The decor was upscale, barely fit for flip-flops. This being Kauai, though, none of the diners was wearing a tie. I'd have thought ties were banned on island if I hadn't seen the waitstaff and bartender wearing them myself.

A few older guys sat at the bar, staring down their drinks. Vacationing couples took up most of the tables, gazing into one another's eyes. To say nothing was moving fast in the place would be an understatement. The restaurant was as dead as the surf on a day-old beer.

I made eye contact with the barkeep and ordered bourbon neat. He poured before I could change my order but not my mind. I slipped a twenty beside the glass. This whole day—with the Jeeps, Mody pulling a gun and giving me the slip, needing to replace my tires, combined with Gina's ration of shit, *and* Leonardi pushing himself up my ass—led me to stare long and hard into that bourbon. The smell came up and met me halfway. I knew I could do it, that I wasn't losing anything big like a chip or my resolve, but somewhere I had heard that a drink was the acceptance of weakness.

"Everything okay?"

I looked up. The barkeep was right there, wondering if he'd done something wrong.

"You know a guy named Mody?" Joe's talk had put my mind to business. Now I wanted this guy, was willing to try anything.

"Mody? Should I?"

"No. Maybe. Any bells?"

He shook his head, wiped down the bar.

I gave him Gina's name. First and last. "She's looking to collect on a debt from your boss."

His eyes thinned. By how he was sizing me up, I got the idea he was why she wasn't coming back here ever—something about the set of his shoulders, how he rested one arm on the bar. He'd touched her, that I knew.

I wanted to set him straight, but I'd get the money first. He pointed toward the back of the place, where a heavyset chef filled the kitchen window. "The boss back there. Ask him. Tread lightly though, or he'll spit in your food."

I set the bourbon on top of the twenty and made my way back through the place, clenching and opening my fists. Something was building up inside me, and I was half-willing to let it out.

If the couples noticed anything beyond their loved one's eyes, they might've gotten a chill.

The big chef watched me the whole way back, squinting hard—not like he wanted to know me, more like he didn't. The name on his shirt said *Ted*.

"That your name? Ted?"

He was big but soft. A situation ran itself through my head that involved me slamming him around in the back of the place, bouncing him off a few garbage cans or trees, whatever I could find.

Then I saw the size of the guy standing behind him. Easily three hundred pounds of mean-looking Hawaiian sous-chef.

Ted asked, "What's that to you?"

I rolled my tongue along the back of my teeth.

"I want to talk about Gina. This a good time?"

He took a look at the big-boy sous-chef, waved him at me. "Our friend here ain't got no manners. Maybe you show him out."

"I'd like that." I was losing control, some sense of what usually kept me on the rails. Maybe I liked it. The bourbon would've helped, but that was back on the bar. Leonardi was thousands of miles away. Who knew what kind of a police this island had, what they'd be likely to care about, or how long they'd take to answer a call. I didn't know or care. Not right then.

12

Sneakers

I walked through the kitchen door and allowed the sous-chef to show me onto the back deck. "Be right with you," I told Ted. He smiled.

We were all becoming fast friends.

The back side of the place had an elevated porch that overlooked some trees. The sous-chef took off his apron and laid it over the rail. That was when I stepped in and hit him hard with a right hook. It was a little less than gentlemanly to get the jump like that, but I wasn't waiting for him to start in. Still, all my punch did was turn his cheek the other way. He smiled when he looked back at me.

Then he tried grabbing my shirt, which was a mistake. As soon as he touched fabric, I had his hand in mine and twisted his wrist. He wasn't prepared for the speed of it. I had been practicing the moves Chan taught me, and I was getting good at them. My arm-twist turned the chef around, exposing his side and a big gut. I put a knee right up under his sternum, then did it again for good measure. He coughed up his gum onto the deck.

I gave his wrist another twist just to hurt it, not enough to break it. Then I snapped his head back with an uppercut to his nose.

"That's enough."

I turned my head to see Ted standing in the open doorway. He held a big knife.

"Talk," he said. "Tell me what you want."

I held the wrist, checked my man's face. He nodded. It was the equivalent of tapping out. As soon as I let go, he took his apron off the rail, used it to catch the blood coming from his nose.

"We're not fighters here," Ted said. "We make food."

"That wasn't your tune one minute ago." I wrung my hands, cracking knuckles and squeezing the muscles in my palms. "But I'm glad we all learned that lesson. Now put the knife down."

He stepped back into the doorway, set the knife down on something, then stepped out onto the deck, showing me his empty hands.

"Gina sent me," I said. "I'm here for her money."

"Shit," he said. "That bitch? She walked out in the middle of a shift and never came back. What I owe her?"

"She says back pay plus tips."

He swore again, turned to spit a thin stream through his teeth.

"The fuck I care. Here." He pulled out a wad of money held by a rubber band and looked it over, then thumbed out five hundreds and handed them to me. "Give her that and tell her to fuck off. Say the balance goes to damages."

I took the money and thought it over. "She said more."

He waved at the bar. "Bitch broke two bottles, *top shelf*, before leaving and threw a hundred dollars of fish in the river. Tell her to fuck herself."

I weighed the cash in one hand and his words in my head. Both worked better than bringing nothing back to Gina.

Neither of the chefs looked imposing now. I could see the bar inside and the bartender behind it, watching us out of the corner of his eye as he made drinks.

"Make me happy," I said. "Tell me you know how to find a guy named Meyer Mody."

The sous-chef laughed. "Fucking Sneakers? Man, this guy wants Sneakers." He took the apron away from his face and looked at it. The bleeding had stopped.

Ted said, "Shit, M&Ms isn't back on island, is he?" He turned to the sous-chef. "You know M&Ms?"

"Man, everybody know Sneakers. That what *we* call him."

"You sure Mody's back?"

I said, "I saw him today."

The sous-chef made a sour face, spit off the deck into the grass.

Ted nodded. "Round now when the Koloas get too sick a waiting, they looking for him to pay."

"The Koloas?" I asked. "Who?"

"About now they start making trouble for his moms."

I hadn't been able to find anything on Mody's computer about his mother, but that was the kind of thing most people kept hardwired in their memory, didn't write down.

"His mom is here? On the island?" When he seemed to agree, I asked him where.

He grimaced like asking about the location of a guy's mother went too far, but then he shrugged.

"What I care? His mom stays up Waimea. Big place he

bought her a few years back. Back before the trouble with them Jordans."

"Jordans?" I perked up even more. "What Jordans?"

"Oh, man." He laughed. "You ain't heard his story yet? Then you don't know Mody."

The sous-chef shook his head, laughing. "His whole story about those *Maltese Jordans.*"

Ted pointed and smiled. "The *Maltese*," he said. "*That* is his biggest scam. Fucking tried to get me to help front his big purchase. Talking about 'The Legend.'" He waved it off. "Whatever. Told him go to the Koloas."

Now the sous-chef was surprised. "What? You didn't want to take a chance on that?"

"Crazy? Believe what you want. I keep my money."

I was lost. "Is his mother up here in Hanalei?"

Ted clucked. "No, man. She ain't Hanalei. Modys stay up in Waimea. His big house there."

"What's Waimea? Where is it?"

He frowned. "Out past Kekaha his house. Up Mānā Road."

"What?"

It occurred to me that I could just check the island's phonebook for its Modys. Basic investigative footwork from back in the time of landlines, but here, odds were good his mother would actually have one.

The sous-chef said, "You really don't think they was real? His story?"

Ted waved it off and turned back into the kitchen. I pocketed the money and went back into the bar. I waved the bartender over.

"You got a phone book back there?"

He brought it. When he got close, I grabbed his tie, pulled him half-way over to my side.

"You touch Gina?" I said, my face close to his.

"I just asked her out, man. That's it."

I pulled the tie tighter around his neck, jerked it down toward my knees. His mouth smacked into the wood of the bar.

"You sure?"

He made a sound, something like a complaint, with his mouth and tongue checking teeth. I jerked him down again, bounced his face a second time. When he opened his mouth, I saw blood. That was good with me.

I picked up my bourbon and knocked it back. That settled something inside me. Not just the decision to have a drink, but that adrenaline calmed right down. I sucked in air behind it to set the burn with fresh cold.

That was good.

He had his hands on the bar, trying to steady himself if I pulled his tie again. I cupped the short glass in my palm and slammed its bottom down onto his fingers. He pulled his hand away, squirmed and made a kind of yell in the back of his throat. This got all the diners' attention.

Time for me to go.

I left him with a warning not to touch women when they didn't want, pushed him back behind the bar, and took my twenty along with the phonebook.

Ted and his sous-chef stood in the kitchen doorway, watching me leave. If it was me, I wouldn't take well to getting roughed up, but maybe on the island things operated differently.

I hadn't lain eyes on a single cop since I'd landed, if that was any indication. In any case, I didn't stop; I gave the Bar Acuda a break to lick its wounds.

Maybe my big city ass could cruise around doing damage and not get kicked in the teeth. I was hoping as much. It was a nice thought if it held.

If it didn't, I didn't plan to be around.

13

Waimea

Turned out Mody's mom was actually in the phonebook, listed just like a normal person, along with a street address: Pratima Mody on Mānā Road. Leave it to somebody's mother to still have a landline. I was back in the old days: listings, addresses, all there in a book of public access. How easy that made things.

By the map on my iPhone, I saw this would be another long haul, all the way back down to the southern side of the island, even past my hotel. I was sick of the damned main road, but looking up at the high, jagged, green mountains of the island's interior, I knew cutting across wasn't going to happen. Jeep or no Jeep.

So I started on my way. I was making progress, but not without a lot of wear on my tires and ass. If helping Gina with her problem had led me back to something on Mody though, that was a two-bird-one-stone situation. Maybe karma was coming back around to help me. I couldn't complain.

Sneakers. I had to laugh to at that. What else could this guy's nickname be?

By the time I got back down near Poipu, it was past eleven. Part of me wanted to stop in at the hotel and give Gina her cash, get some sleep even, but the bigger part of me wanted Mody and knew I had to get this thing done. Leonardi wouldn't take failure as an option, and now I was starting to feel the clock.

I passed the turn for Poipu and stayed on the highway.

After a time, I passed through a couple small villages with names stuffed full of vowels. They looked like run-down versions of a sixties beach town.

From there, I found Kekaha and followed my phone's directions onto a road that brought me north, then started a gentle climb heading directly away from the ocean—or as direct as any winding, ambling island road can go.

As I drove up, the terrain changed: first I passed through grassy lowlands with few trees. Then I climbed above that and the road paralleled the ocean, overlooking the dark water in the night. A big yellow moon hung far out on the horizon, making the waves shimmer.

I drove on. Here were bigger houses, cars parked along the sides of the road, trees in yards. The address looked to be pretty far along. But what did I know—of the island, of distances, of anything about this place?

I finally found the house close to midnight and parked across the street. I had to double check the number on the mailbox with the address I'd put in my phone. This house was unlike anything I'd yet seen on Kauai. Mody must have had it built, or somebody did, and not long ago. It had cost a fancy penny.

Practically the whole façade was windows facing the ocean. It's what I would have wanted if privacy was not an issue. What walls the place had were either glass or stark white. Inside, a big central staircase wound up the front of the great room to a second-floor balcony. An impressive chandelier hung above this, filled with as many glass pieces as I could imagine. All the lights inside the place were off. So far as I could tell, the whole house was dark.

And still I could see inside, almost as if the house glowed. The couch, the tables, the kitchen—everything I saw inside was white. White. *White.* Whatever moonlight made it up this far helped, but the house had something about it, too.

Now I knew where the money went. Where it would most likely continue going. Mody was a man who took care of his mother. Nothing wrong with that, but this place was more than he could afford.

I tossed Gina's cash into the glove box and locked it—not that that made it safe, but better there than with me—and stepped out of the Jeep, crunching a few pebbles along the road. I saw a minivan in the drive and a big Toyota Tacoma parked just up the street. The Tacoma looked like it got driven off road a lot, through mud and a lot worse. It had miles of extra suspension.

If Mrs. Mody was here, she wasn't alone.

I went around to the back of my Jeep and found the tire iron. It made as good a weapon as any and had good weight to it, especially in the head.

I took a few deep breaths to collect myself. I could see out past the ocean. Here on the island, with a lack of big-city lights, I could see far more stars than usual, make out the Milky Way and beyond: to the far reaches of the universe. The stars stretched on forever in constellations, solar systems, whatever else you could call them.

Once my breathing was steady, I turned to the house for a better look. Crossing the street, I saw a single light shining on the side of the house, out behind the driveway. There, on the side of the house, I saw another vehicle; as I got closer, I could tell it was a Jeep. The Jeep. Mody was here.

I crept across the street. If Mack and Mody were both in the house, if it was possible I could get that lucky, I'd put a hurt on them both.

He'd still have the gun, and that upped the danger. But guns weren't new to me anymore, and staring down a barrel was starting to feel like part of my new life, complete with the thoughts that nagged me afterward to make a change. And here I was. At the very least, a gun coming into play made me worth everything Leonardi shelled out.

Up the front path, I walked toward the house, coming to an enclosed entry just off center. Here was a wide set of double doors and a shining button for the bell. Just that easy: ring and wait. That was all I had to do.

Really.

Instead I stood still. I knew better than to ring that bell. I just listened, heard crickets, like a summer night anywhere, and wind rushing through the trees.

Then I heard something crash from inside—upstairs, I thought. Glass broke. I didn't hear anyone yelling or making noise, but something was going down. There I was, standing at the front door with a tire iron in my fist.

I tried the knob. It turned and the door opened.

I walked inside.

14

Shark Mode

The house was much darker inside than I expected. Perhaps the glass had a tint to it, a glaze to keep out the sun.

I heard something else break upstairs, then yelling.

I closed the door with as little sound as I could manage, looked left and right, then started up the stairs in front of me. Off to my left, something moved in the kitchen and then was gone. I chose to keep moving ahead. When in doubt, do what a shark would do and swim forward. That's generally an effective working principle, I've found.

At the top of the stairs, I saw a set of double doors and another door, a single, off to the left. I chose the doubles, going straight in. Shark mode. Shark week, in fact—if I lived that long.

The knob on the right door turned easily. I heard deep voices inside and knew I had a lot more to fear than finding Mody's mom inside naked.

What I saw when I went in was two big dudes, guys who looked like former body builders gone soft a little, standing over a bed where a middle-aged couple had the covers pulled up to their chins.

Around the bed were a few smashed bedside lamps.

One of body builders turned toward me. "The fuck is this?"

If I was betting, my money said these were the Koloa brothers I'd heard about. I kept the tire iron low behind my back. Maybe with a little surprise, I might come out on top of things.

The brother closest to me made his move; he stormed in my direction like an offensive tackle trying to get outside and block for a screen. I faked left and went at him low, cracking his shin with the iron. He winced and moved past, hopping up onto one leg to hold the spot that I'd hit. Nothing was broken, but he'd feel it for a while. I watched him for a next move, figuring if I should try to take out his other leg. He stayed where he was, though, then nodded toward the bed and his other brother.

The second brother looked pissed. I noticed then that he was the bigger of the two. Bigger and maybe meaner. He grunted and started toward me slowly, lowering his center of gravity like a sumo wrestler. I swung the iron, but he just raised a meaty forearm and took it right below his elbow. After that, he got inside on me and lifted me off my feet, and then we both went down onto the bed, on top of Mom and Dad, hard. I could feel their limbs flailing under me, and the supports inside the bed gave out. We all felt the bed drop to the floor, then everyone's arms and legs were scrambling and clinging and hitting at one another.

"Come on," I said, but more to the world than anyone in particular.

Kicks and punches landed all over my body, some hard and some soft. Blankets and pillows were everywhere.

I managed to roll myself off the bed and onto the floor. I turned in time to see my assailant punch the old man in the face.

Mr. Mody, or whoever he was, went immediately still.

The brother behind me said, "Johnny, Jesus. Not the old man."

Mody's mother went berserk, swinging her arms every which way, pummeling the big guy. He reared back, and I took the moment when he was surprised and off balance to launch myself at his body. My shoulder hit him from the side and knocked him off the bed, onto the floor. When he looked up, I threatened with the tire iron, hoping he wouldn't make me use it unsuccessfully a second time.

I stepped back toward the wall, protecting my blind side, but when I turned I saw the first brother still standing where he was, shocked by what had just happened.

He came to his senses and said, "We're sorry for that, Mr. Mody, Mrs. Mody. Nothing meant by it."

The old man looked knocked out. I wouldn't be surprised.

"The hell are you thugs doing in my bedroom," Mrs. Mody said. "Go on and get out!"

The second brother, the one called Johnny, got up to his feet. He regarded me as a nuisance. "Who the fuck are you? And why you here, haole?"

"I'm looking for Mody," I said, "just like everybody else."

"What did he do?"

I asked her, "Where's your son, ma'am? Is Meyer even here?"

Mrs. Mody was a small Indian woman. She pulled the sheets back up over her body. "Meyer is not home now. As far as I know, he is not even on the island. What in the name of Ganesh did he do to start this business?" Mrs. Mody didn't have an ounce of denial in her. She stared at me like she already knew the answer. And if the money was a bond or a loan, it didn't matter. I could see a long pattern playing out over decades through the look on her face.

She shook her head. "I told him we didn't need this much house."

I started to say something but didn't have the heart. Maybe Mody and Mack weren't even here. Now these extra larges were going to be my problem too, if I kept going in this direction.

I asked them, "He owe you money? Is that it?"

The bigger brother supported the one with the hurt shin. "Oh, shit. He don't even know about the J's, Eddie." He grimaced at me. "The fuck you doing here?"

The one he'd called Eddie tried his foot, stepping softly to avoid more pain in the shin. "Fuck this guy," he said. "I wanna kill him."

I said, "Are you talking about the Jordans?"

"Shit, haole. Yes, the Jordans. Mody saying he got the ones he always talk about. The ultimate. *The* kicks. *They ones*. Them ones he calls the *Maltese*."

Eddie took a ginger step toward me. "You give us what he owes. Start with whatever you holding."

That was when the bedroom door opened and a third brother stepped in, this one bigger than the first two. They all looked alike, so much so that they had to be brothers, whether Koloa or not. The first two nodded at him, and one said, "Doc."

Doc took my measure, head to foot. "So who are you then?"

"I'm—" And I was stuck. They knew I was looking for Mody, but not who I was or where I came from. And I liked it that way.

"We know you?"

"No." These guys didn't look like the sharpest tools in the chest, and I didn't want to start giving them any ideas. "Listen, let me just be going." I waved an apology at Mrs. Mody, hoping she'd get through the night.

"Yeah, no. I don't think so." Eddie reached for my arm. I half-expected it, too. What kind of gangster would let someone walk out in a situation like this? Finally, some things on Kauai were starting to make sense. Not that it helped me.

When I stepped away, I bumped into the third brother, Doc, who had closed in fast. He caught me around the arms and held me in a grip like a car-crusher. The tire iron fell to the floor.

"Fuck me," I said. "Really? You dudes want some more?"

"Yeah." Eddie and Johnny nodded.

Then Doc said, "I'm going to put him down those stairs."

15

Fourth Down

The brother called Doc carried me out of the bedroom, the one called Eddie following us, favoring his right leg. Back in the bedroom, I heard Johnny talking, then Mrs. Mody answering in rapid clips.

Out on the landing, I went along for the ride, seeing how far it would go, not that I had much choice. We reached the top of the staircase, a kind of tipping point, and Doc summarily tossed me. He tossed me handily, I should say, and suddenly I found myself in the air staring down that beautiful glass and metal staircase.

"Shit."

I hit the steps with my shoulder and rolled, bounced off a clear plexi siding built into the railings that I'd need to thank somebody for later. Tumbling off the stairs and through the air would've been far worse.

I half-rolled and half-fell around the curve of the staircase, somersaulting more times than a guy my age would want, but protecting my head and ultimately not making a mess of my body on the way down.

I landed on my ass at the bottom, rolled to my feet, and

sprung up as best I could. Nothing broken, only some things creaky. My back felt okay. Eddie and Doc had already started down after me.

"Come on," I told them. "Bring it."

Now that tiger blood was kicking through my veins again, I wanted the fight. I set both feet and raised my fists.

Doc was the first down but had no idea what he was doing, unless a new brand of island-style fighting involves jumping down the last three steps of a staircase. He brought the flying body tackle back from an old WWF playbook, but made the mistake of leaving his feet before he knew where he'd land. Any high school ballplayer knows you should never do that. There, stretched out sideways like I would catch him or let him flatten me, I saw his face go slack when he realized I could still move out of the way.

And that's what I did.

I took a step back so I was out of reach. He tried to right himself, leaned to get his legs back under him, but barely made it. His feet hit at an awkward angle, and I faked a kick to sweep them out from under. When he saw that coming, he put all of his concentration— what hadn't already been directed there—into maintaining his balance. That left his head wide open for my biggest right hook. I stepped in and lit him up from the opposite direction, basically caught him leaning all his weight into my punch. When my fist hit his temple, I could feel his skull cave slightly to the simple physics of two objects in opposition trying to keep their inertia.

He shook, stopped still on both feet, wobbled, and still didn't cover himself, so I brought a quick left hook then a right uppercut that closed his jaw with a clack. If he'd been wagging his tongue, he'd have lost it.

After that, he was basically out on his feet, meaning he was done but for some reason didn't go down. Maybe these brothers were tough or something.

Eddie had stopped halfway down the stairs. He whistled and I looked up.

"Okay, Jack Palms, no more fighting." He held a little grey revolver, maybe a Combat Magnum, and that stopped me cold. I was starting to feel like the A-Team, always bringing my fists to a gun fight, waiting for the scene at the end of the show where we got to duke it out. Only this wasn't a show, people actually used their guns, and I needed to seriously reconsider my priorities about carrying one.

I held my hands up. "You don't really want to use that, do you? Let's just call this evening over and agree to find Mody on our own. Okay?"

"Your movies sucked."

I backed toward the front door. Doc sat down abruptly on the steps.

"Okay." I kept my hands high. "Who you now? Some kind of critic?"

"Just fuck you, man. Fuck you and shut the fuck up, bitch."

I didn't say anything to that. Apparently our moment of decorum had ended.

Johnny appeared above us. He snapped his fingers. "Knew I recognized him from somewhere. Welcome back from the eighties, haole."

Eddie shrugged. "I just figured out where I knew him from. Kind of funny."

I watched his gun, felt my heel hit the welcome mat behind me. I reached for the door.

Johnny said, "Show him out, Eddie."

"Fuck yourself, Jack. This our island. Our business."

I knew the right thing to do was to just get out, make like they were saying and go. "I have business with Mody."

Eddie whistled again like I had either impressed or disappointed him. I couldn't decide which.

Doc gathered himself to his feet. He came at me, pushed me in my chest, and knocked me back against the door. "You heard my brother," he said. "Time for you to be out. Get the fuck gone." He stared me down, still tough after his time out.

The four of us stood there. No one moving.

Then Eddie waved the gun at the door, and I did like I was told. Sometimes you just have to drop back and punt.

16

The Long Goodbye

Outside, I drove my Jeep up the street. When I was far enough away that I couldn't see the house, and I was sure no one could see me from it, I pulled over and shut off the car.

Something told me Mody was still in that house, hiding, waiting. If the brothers were trying to collect money from him and he had it—stolen from San Francisco—I wasn't sure why he'd come all this way and not pay, but then his mother had said something about the house. Maybe his priority was to the bank, not the Koloas. I probably would have gone the same way, though having a roof over your mother's head looked a whole lot worse if visits from thugs like those became frequent.

Times like these—waiting in the night, killing time for the next thing to happen—were when I still missed smoking. I patted myself down, even checked the compartment between the seats, knowing there was no way I'd find a pack. So I leaned back and searched the sky for shooting stars. As soon as I knew I could count on the Koloas being gone, I was going back to the house.

Instead of smoking, I counted breaths, a trick I had picked up from Chan and his meditation. I tried to make each breath go slow, counting the inhale and the exhale, stretching and contracting my ribcage. What adrenaline I'd had from the fight started to seep away, and eventually things began to slow.

When I got to one hundred breaths, I started up the car and turned around. Sure enough, the Toyota Tacoma was gone. This time I parked on the front lawn and left my lights on, the engine running.

I jumped out and went right through the front door.

"Okay, Mody," I yelled. "Get your ass out here. *Now!*"

When no one made a noise, I waited. Then, after a couple of minutes, I called Mack's name, then Mody's name again. "Get the fuck out here!"

I said, "I've got a gun, and if you don't come out and show yourself, I'm going to do one worse than those idiots and go up the stairs to start shooting mothers." I listened for a few seconds. "You wouldn't want *that*, would you?"

Then I heard some kind of cabinet or compartment opening in the kitchen. It made a scratching sound and I heard footsteps and then I could see Mody standing in what little light the kitchen had to offer.

There in the flesh: Meyer Mody himself. Just a little guy, hardly worth all of this trouble.

"Fuck *me*," I said. "You left those idiots alone with your parents?"

Mody lifted his shoulders and let them fall. "He's not my actual dad."

I couldn't believe what I was hearing. Now the sneakers weren't the only thing that felt like I was dealing with teenagers.

"Pack your shit. We're going back to the mainland. You're going to jail."

At that, Mack stepped out of the compartment Mody had been hiding in. He held a gun, the same one I'd seen that morning, the nickel-plated .45. Now, as before, it was pointed at me.

"You sure about that?" he said.

"I am." I was beyond tired of people pointing guns at me. It had grown old and then some.

I stepped across the room fast and at an angle. Mack barely kept the gun on me. I've learned you either mean to do something with a gun and do it, or you don't and just talk. He hadn't fired yet, so I put him in the second camp. Pretty much everyone on this island was in that camp, so far as I saw. Time to fish or cut bait. If someone clipped me with a bullet, I'd get through it. I'd been through worse.

But if someone was going to put lead in me, it sure as shit wouldn't be Mack.

I came right in on him and knocked his arm, sending the gun toward the windows. Then I hit him in the mouth and cranked the gun out of his hand.

Mody had both hands above his shoulders when I turned his way.

"Either of you try any shit like that again, we're done being pals."

He just stared.

"Fucking guns. I'm sick of this shit." I pushed Mack across the room toward Mody. "You want to say goodbye to your mother before we leave?"

"Jack, let me tell you—

I cut him off. "What'd you do with that money? How you

get in like this with those guys? They the Koloas?"

He shrugged, which I took for a yes. Then he spread his hands. Before he could start on some bullshit explanation, I said, "Where are the Jordans? Do they even exist?"

"Oh, they sure do, Jack. Oh, man! You *have to* see them."

"Tell Joe Leonadri. He holds your bond back in San Francisco, where we're going."

I walked him upstairs, the gun in the back of my pants but ready. Mack lumbered behind. I was done with them both, but Mody's mother and step-dad seemed like the salt of the earth, the sort who deserved some basic courtesy. So I let their son say goodbye.

He promised his mom he'd be back from the mainland soon and that he'd stay longer next time.

He didn't mention jail—that he'd been or was going—and I didn't raise the point. Minimizing his familial damage was the least I could do.

When we got outside, I told Mack to fuck off. Mody's rented Jeep was still parked in the drive and he could take it. As soon as he found the keys, that is; I threw them into the bushes behind the house.

"Good luck with that."

Mody said, "Hey, come on, man! That's a rental. You know what happens if I don't bring that thing back? What that'll cost me?" He gave me a hard look, one that didn't have anything behind it.

Mack went to start looking among the leaves.

I had Mody drive my Jeep back to the Sheraton while I sat in back giving him directions. He knew the way, but I liked him to do what I said, and for him to feel the barrel of a gun to his skull.

Given what he'd put me through, he wasn't getting any more chances.

Back at the Sheraton, I took Mody around back to the beach side and up the outside stairs to my floor instead of going through the main lobby. I didn't want Gina or anybody in the restaurant to see me. I'd had enough problems with that. And keeping Mody away from people helped discourage him from running. I kept my hand on his arm, so he wouldn't take a chance that I might not pull the gun in front of people. I wouldn't, but I'd happily run him down and knock the shit out of him if I had to.

Up in my room, I pulled the sheets off the bed, rolled them up, then used them to tie his arms and legs to a chair. He complained the whole time.

When he was secure, I grabbed my laptop, fired it up, and twenty minutes later I had us booked on the first flight to San Francisco in the morning.

All I had to do now was get through the night.

I sent down for a bottle of whiskey, two hamburgers and some club soda. We'd start with that and then move on to coffee when it got closer to sunrise.

Part II

The Shoes

All I wanted was them Jordans with the blue suede on 'em.

17

The Maltese Jordans

I ate a hamburger watching Mody stare at the TV. He tried talking to me, but I offered to shut him up with a pillowcase in his mouth if he kept at it. I didn't want to hear anything until after I ate.

When I had a whiskey and soda in my hand and food in my stomach, I offered him a drink, but he declined.

"How much do you want to let me go?" he asked. "To leave me on the island and just go away. I'm serious. I'll pay you double whatever *he* is. How much?"

I took a good sip, chewing a small piece of ice. "Who's he?" I asked. "You don't even know."

He bit his upper lip. "Listen, Jack. It's Jack Palms, right? I seen your movies. You're good. Or you were, at least. *Now* who the fuck are you?"

I had Mody tied to a chair, and I'd been eating at the desk. I moved to the bed, sitting on its edge in front of the TV. "I'm turning this up now," I said, taking the remote in my hand.

"Money, Jack. Listen, I'm talking money. However much you want."

"More than you've got. I just want to get this job done."

"Listen," he said. "No." He leaned forward as far as the bed sheets tied around his arms would let him. "You don't get it. I have something invaluable. *Everyone* wants this. It's once in a *lifetime*."

"What's that?"

"A pair. *The pair*. Sneakers. I'm talking about a ghost pair of Michael Jordan's kicks that have only been rumored to exist. One of one here, Jack. Never been made but this pair. And *he* wore them."

"The Maltese Jordans?" I was only repeating what I'd heard Ted say at the Bar Acuda, but it made Mody's face light up like a kid at Christmas.

"Shit. Yes! They're real. Official. I have them *and* I have the proof."

I took another drink, put the remote down, the volume still on low. I eyeballed Mody, trying to gauge his level of BS.

"Ask me," he said. "Ask me what they are."

"Like the book," I said. "Dashiell Hammett?"

"Yeah. Like the book, but that's only the tagline I came up with. It's a good book, but these have an even better story." He smiled wide. "They're the *Rara shoevis numero uno.* Dig?"

"No. Not really."

"But these are *real!* Saudi Arabia, money!"

I wasn't sure if he was calling me "money" like Mars Blackmon did in the commercials, or if he meant the ability of Saudis to fund an insane sneaker collector's wet dream of an enterprise.

"Like something his Airness wore in a dunk contest?"

Mody laughed. "Not even close."

"An All-Star appearance? A finals game?" I was starting to bite. My basketball fandom and its subsequent curiosity, my suppressed love of sneakers was getting the better of me.

"Not those, either. What do you think would be *the* most exquisite and unique pair of Jordans out there. Signed, game-worn, whatever. Imagine the most far-out thing you can dream up and then multiply that by ten."

"What?"

He raised his shoulders toward his ears, waiting. Now he was enjoying himself. I could tell. "Guess. This is part of the fun."

"The sixty-three-point game against the Celtics in his first playoffs, the one when Larry Bird called him 'God.'"

"No, Bird said it was 'God disguised as Michael Jordan.' Let's not misquote Bird here."

"So they're from that game?"

Through pursed lips, he said, "Nope. Try again. That's really not even close."

"His first game in Jordans? The first pair of Jordans he ever wore?"

"Nice. Those would be great. But there's no story there. If those exist, none of us has ever heard of them. Maybe they're not even still out there." He raised one finger. "You have to remember, back in the beginning, no one even knew who this kid would be. I mean, maybe Phil Knight guessed right about him, but this was just a kid from North Carolina named Michael back then.

"Plus, the grail of all Jordans is the Elevens, not the ones. These just happen to be the greatest model of Jordan sneaker Tinker ever made, signed by MJ *and* him, *and* they're an exclusive, one-of-a-kind that Nike never even produced, officially.

"So, more extravagant, Jack. Think of a game that wasn't even played on an NBA court."

"*Space Jam*! The kicks MJ wore when he played with Bugs and Taz and all that shit?"

"No fucking way. Those would be *devalued* for something like that. What a piece of shit that movie was."

"But still, those would be valuable, right?"

"Yes. Absolutely. But not like these. Enough guessing. Let me tell you a story." His eyes, his face were cold. He had the most serious look I'd seen on him yet. This meant that much to him.

I went to the desk and got the whiskey bottle, brought it back to the bed and poured myself three fingers, then set the bottle on the floor.

"Okay," I said. "Tell me."

"Jordan's contract," Mody started, "his 'love of the game' clause. You know what that means?"

I nodded. "Something about playing anytime, anywhere he wanted. They couldn't stop him."

He nodded. "Good. No, they couldn't stop him from playing the game he loved. Not anywhere or with anyone. But. *But*, what they didn't figure on was that this would be for games that he just wanted to get into. Summer league, playing with friends, pickup, whatever. They never expected he'd need the money and want to play for anyone else. Not for pay."

"Why would he need money?" I started to speculate about his gambling habits, what had reportedly been a huge financial problem during a big part of his career. Some even thought it had led to his father's murder.

"Let's just say, he needed big money at a time when his career was in jeopardy, money that he couldn't go to the bank for or get as an advance from the Bulls. The timing just worked out: wrong for him, right for the confluence of events that needed to happen to create the perfect storm for making these shoes."

I said, "You have my attention."

"Good," Mody said. "Good. So, of course he couldn't play for any other *teams*, not in the world, in any league, not anything like that. That's not what I'm saying. This isn't Virtus Bologna or some Italian or Euro team with a lot of money. No, this is *crazy money*. Like nothing anyone has ever heard of for a single game."

"A million dollars? What's that to him?" I had no ideas. I showed him my hands. "What?"

"The King of Malta," he said. "I'm talking about one man. A shitload of cash. National riches. One game. Totally unsanctioned, un-televised, completely off the grid. The king and four of his men against Jordan and the Maltese B-Squad. An exhibition purely for the crown. The stuff of myth and legend. Rare air.

"And for this game? One pair. Specialized and then gifted to the king. These are *the Pair* we are talking about, Jack. Jordan-worn for one game, overseas, totally clandestine and secret. Played in once for *a lot* of money. A game you know he won."

"So what? Who would believe this? You made it up?"

"No." He shook his head. "Years later, a video surfaced. Copied, pirated, who knows, but it shows up, clips of it. Websites. Jordan playing with the Maltese B-squad. Unquestionably him. The kicks are real. The video shows him signing this exact pair with the king himself. And Tinker right there, too."

"Tinker? Who's that?"

"Tinker Hatfield. He's the guy at Nike who designed the Jordans—Three through Fifteen and then Twenty and a couple others that don't matter. Sneaker legend. Royalty of the kicks. You with me?"

I was.

"Later, the Jordans came to light. After losing favor in his parliament, a few years after that, the King of Malta sells them to pay off his debts. He's living in exile. He's got a certificate of authenticity for the kicks signed by Jordan himself."

"You're serious. The *Maltese Jordans*?"

He smiled even wider. "Exactly. Like Dashiell Hammett, Jack. Doesn't that make it even more beautiful? Dating all the way back to the 1990s."

"That's bullshit. You know that's bullshit, right?"

Now he laughed. "Yes!" He laughed harder. "You know it is."

I breathed a heavy sigh of relief.

"It's a joke," he said.

"I thought so."

"It was actually Saudi Arabia," he said. He smiled, but not like he was laughing. More like he was crazy. His teeth showed all the way back to his molars.

"What?"

"Come on, Jack. Malta has been its own country since 1974. And even before that, the last reigning king wasn't a king, it was Queen Elizabeth. Duh."

"Are you fucking serious?"

"Don't you know your colonies? Malta broke away from the United Kingdom in 1964. Its head of state is the *President* of

Malta. Actually Vincent Tabone at the time of all this. But that doesn't matter. Google it."

I took a long drink of the scotch. I was starting to need it.

He shook his head in agreement. "Tabone is bullshit. I'm fucking with you. I just like saying his name. The president at the time of all this, I *freaking* testify on my testicles, was his successor, Ugo Mifsud Bonnici." He cupped his groin as if to offer it up to God or lightning if he was wrong.

I was starting to have no idea what I should be following or believing.

"Sorry, man. I've just been telling this story for so long that I've added a few side-flourishes. Makes it fun for me. Anyway, I swear to you I'm back on truth. The President of Malta was Ugo Mifsud Bonnici, which also doesn't matter, but I like saying his name, too. This was in late summer of 1996.

"As far as the sneakers are concerned, man, come on. Saudi Arabia. That's where the real money is. That's the king. The Saudi part is implied. No one would ever think something this amazing would come out of Malta. Malta is tiny. It's like nothing. Except for Hammett. There's that, of course. Literary reference and all."

He tipped his head toward the bottle. "How about you give me a pull off that scotch there, Jack."

I thought about untying him to drink it, but didn't give that a second to linger. I poured two fingers into a glass and held it to his mouth for a drink. He wasn't going to get any sleep on me, and I was actually starting to enjoy where the conversation was going—if only for entertainment.

"So you're saying someone believed all this shit?"

He hummed an objection through the scotch, shaking his head. "No, Jack. This is real. It's not just me and the Koloas. This thing goes to New York and across the Atlantic to Paris and London. God's truth: it's been certified."

I took a drink myself. I needed it. "So the Saudis brought Jordan over for a game. They should've played it in Jordan, just for the fuck of it."

"Right. First time I heard that one." He gave me a sour look.

"*Anyway*, the Saudi king at the time is Fahd. Fahd is a *huge* fan of basketball. Has watched it his whole life, from back in the Mikan days through Russell, Wilt, Big O, Clyde, The Doctor, Magic, and Bird. All of them. He's never seen anyone play like Jordan. Freaking loves him. Can't believe the guy. All-Universe talent.

"And this all gets crazy when Jordan comes back from baseball. Fahd thinks it is *literally* the second coming, which it is after that 95–96 season. 72–10. The Jordan Elevens, classic Tinker Hatfield, best sneakers ever, best record ever, freaking Bulls only lose three games in the whole *playoffs* on their way to the title. Fahd just goes flipping crazy.

"And this dude's got *Money*. Capital M, Jack. He brings over Jordan, Tinker, even pays off Phil Knight to let Tinker design a special pair of Jordans just for him for this one game. They're based off the Elevens, mostly just a slight modification, but remember this was back before any changing in the basic style or *anything*. Not reissues, player exclusives, none of that. This is the time of *originals*. Just a few colorways and that's it."

"Did he?"

"What? Design the sneakers?" He nodded. "They came up

with some special colors: beige and gold. And you know where the Elevens have patent leather on them? Turned it to gold leaf. Real gold leaf on a Goddamned sneaker!"

I sat dead still, tried to imagine playing a game in sneakers covered in real gold leaf. It wasn't easy, but I could *see* them. The gold: shiny, flaky. Like a shard of mica you could peel chips off of and admire the sparkle.

Mody just kept going. "They added fucking jewels to the upper, rubies and emeralds and shit they thought the king would like. You imagine? They're not even that wild-looking. Truly, amazing.

"Anyway, *these* are the kicks: beige and *gold leaf* Elevens, jewel encrusted, worn by Jordan in Saudi Arabia for one totally illegal, completely unsanctioned game, signed by Jordan *and* Hatfield, each, on *both* sneakers. Fucking mint condition, too. You know Jordan didn't have to work hard to beat the King's squad."

He sat back, clearly satisfied with himself, and asked for more scotch. I took a sip instead, then sat there chewing ice, staring at him.

"You want to know more about the game?" he asked. "Who the king brought in to play Jordan? Shit. King's not going to pay all this money for a nothing-nobody game. He brings in Alaa Abdelnaby from Duke, *Kareem himself* and a young kid named God Shammgod from Providence. Dude likes the deity-type names. You know what I'm saying. Throw in a dude known as Ron Artest from St. John's at the time and the king's squad was pretty dope.

"So what's he do? Jordan runs their shit. Remember, he's just come off a sick season, arguably his best ever. NBA *and* Finals

MVP. This is your boy. Give him four guys with two arms, two legs—which is basically what the Saudi B-Squad was—and he's gonna win it. That's MJ. That's just him."

Part of me didn't care if any of this was true. Part of me *wanted* it to be true and to see the sneakers, and part of me just wanted to bring this idiot back to Leonardi, collect on the bond, and get it all the fuck over with.

He kept looking at me, waiting for an answer. An answer to what?

I pushed a plate of French fries toward him. "You hungry?"

He looked at the fries with disdain. "Not for that. You want to order me some real food and untie me, I could use a last poke bowl if we're really heading back to the mainland."

I wasn't about to go out for him, and I didn't want to order down for more room service. I'd done it once and that hadn't brought Gina, but calling back down there and asking for them to deliver something else was looking for more trouble than I wanted. She'd still be pissed about something, even with some cash in her pocket. It was a situation I'd have to handle, but I wasn't eager to. On the other hand, I couldn't really go back home with her cash from Ted.

"Eat the fries," I said. "Be happy to have those."

He turned his nose up, actually made a show of doing it. I set it on the bed. Then he nodded at the bottle. "How about another pull of that scotch?"

I checked the bottle: I wasn't going to finish it before morning and didn't plan on bringing it back with me. I poured him two fingers into a hotel glass and set it next to the TV.

"Do you promise that if I untie one arm you won't be a pain

in the ass or cause any shit?"

He nodded. "Come on, Jack."

"Seriously. I will fuck you up. I promise."

I untied his left hand and let him hold the scotch. He sipped at it, then slugged it back and asked for more. I poured. He nodded at the fries, so I handed them over.

After a couple of minutes, I put on the TV. Mody's story was still playing around in my head, but I wanted something to look at so I didn't have to watch him staring at me. He was waiting me out, letting the tale about Jordan and Malta and the Saudis play its tricks. I had to admit, I was not immune. And we both knew exactly what he was doing, what was at stake if I bit on the hook.

There was a surfing competition on TV: endless big waves rolling into tubes and young guys on little surfboards carving it up like they were fancy-cutting a watermelon. It relaxed me. I might have fallen asleep after a while, if it weren't for the banging on the door.

I heard my name called through the wood. Gina.

"You in there, Jack? I'm only on break for like fifteen minutes."

"Who's that?" Mody lifted his eyebrows, smiled like he was ready to enjoy a ride. I shut the TV off, got up, and started for the door.

"You alone in there, Jack?"

I said I was coming. I also knocked off the rest of my drink and chewed through some ice before opening the door.

18

Prove It

Gina walked in as soon as the door was open.

"Who the hell is this?" she asked. Among all possible reactions to seeing a guy tied up in my room, this was one I could live with.

"Call him my work."

She gave me the crazy-LA-actor-guy look. "Don't tell me you're into some kinky shit."

"I'm not."

"Did you get the money?"

I dug into my pocket for the stack of bills. "I went to see your old boss. Drove all the way up to Hanalei to do it. He wasn't happy about it, but I actually got you some money."

"That's great." I thought she might kiss, me, but she was waiting for one thing first: the stack.

It wasn't in my right pocket. I tried the left and then patted my back pockets, too.

"Shit."

"What?"

I looked at Mody, who was smiling, and at Gina standing there tapping her foot, waiting for me to fuck it all up—or not.

"The money's downstairs in the Jeep."

"You left eight hundred dollars in a Jeep?" she asked. "That might not be a lot to you, Jack, but for me that's going-home money."

I winced a little, knowing I'd be telling her I got less than the eight hundred. "Don't worry," I said. "It's locked in the glove box."

"Why would I worry?" She turned to Mody. "Should I be worried? Do I look worried?"

He said, "No. Actually, you don't."

"Good. Does he?"

Mody laughed. Gina stood in front of me like a spring ready to pop—right in my face.

"Fuck me," I said. I crossed the room to the bedside table, where I had left the gun right next to a Bible. I shoved the gun down the back of my pants.

Gina said, "The shit is *that*?"

"You know what I do if anything goes wrong here," I said to Mody. I took a few moments to stare him down, making sure he knew I was serious. "Really."

"I get it," he said. The fries were almost done. I took the plate away from him and set it on the other side of the TV. Then I started retying his hand to the chair.

"I'm going to have to ask you to watch him while I go downstairs," I said to Gina. "*Do not* let him get untied or go anywhere, please."

She shifted her weight onto one leg, rested one hand on a hip. "You're not going to leave me with him."

"Do you want the gun?"

"What? Are you crazy?"

It was a bad decision, but that's what I faced all around. I was groping for the lesser of two evils: If I took her down to the car, Mody was alone, with or without the sheets to keep him tied up, and if I asked her to go down, she was alone in a dark parking lot with five hundred in cash.

"Would you rather go down and get the money?" What else could I say? I was willing to try it either way, really. Take my chances on one option or the other.

"Where is it?"

"In the parking lot downstairs. Just like all the others." I took the keys out of my pocket and showed her the license plate info on the tag. What more could I do? "It's silver. A hardtop."

"Jesus, Jack. Just go down with her, already."

Gina nodded. "Right? What the fuck is the matter with this guy?"

I wanted to beat the shit out of Mody. If I knew one thing, it was that I wasn't leaving him alone. "Unh-unh. You do not leave my sight."

"Then I guess we're all going down then, aren't we?" He looked happier than I'd seen him since he left me on the beach.

"Fuck you." I smacked him across the cheek with an open hand, then pointed my finger right between his eyes. "You know what happens if you try anything here?"

He moved his tongue around in his mouth, probably tasting blood. "Come on, Jack. You think I would do that? Besides, I haven't told you the best part of the story yet."

I turned to Gina and then back to Mody. Both of them looked ready to conspire against me, but I didn't know what else I could do.

I showed Mody the gun. "You know what I do with this, right?"

Gina asked, "What *are* you going to do with that? Why do you even have it?"

She had a point. I wouldn't gain anything by shooting Mody, especially if it happened in the hotel or its parking lot. Even if I only maimed him, that'd make it one hell of a lot harder to get him onto an airplane in the morning, which was still my goal. No, I had to keep him in sight *and* restrain him physically if he tried anything.

I swore again, tucked the gun down the back of my pants, and started to untie the sheets around Mody's feet. "You're an asshole," I told him.

Mody laughed to himself as I got his feet untied and then started in on his arms. I could have just cut the linens off, but I wanted to be able to use them again to restrain him. That, and I didn't see any reason for Joe Leonardi to get charged for them.

"Listen, Gina," I said, when I stood up. Mody rose slowly, shaking out his hands and feet to restart his circulation. "About the money."

"He stiffed you, didn't he? What'd he give you? Half?" She opened the door, staring through me like I was made out of smoke. I had to give her some credit; she wasn't far from the truth.

I grabbed the back of Mody's neck and pushed him toward the door. "Let's just go down and count it."

I marched Mody down the hall to the elevator and then stood right next to him as we rode down to the lobby. There the three of us walked out past the valets, and both of them noticed Gina.

They knew her, but were scared off from the look on her face. I'd have been. Neither of them said a word.

She stopped at the top of the turnabout and waited for me to direct her. I pointed to the left. So far Mody was playing it cool, not doing anything rash. I figured if he was going to do anything, he'd likely run for it once we got to the cars. He'd be on the beach in less than a hundred yards. I couldn't let him out of my sight. So I grabbed his arm. I twisted his wrist and brought the arm behind his back.

"Ow!" he said.

"That's nothing," I said. "You want to feel pain, you try something. See what happens."

I handed Gina the keys and directed her toward the Jeep. I was keeping a lookout for Mack or the Extra Large Brothers, though they shouldn't have been able to follow us, for all I knew. Still, I didn't want to leave myself open to surprises.

"It's in the glove box," I said, pointing at the Jeep with my chin when we got close enough. "Use the key."

She used the button to unlock the doors and then leaned in and fumbled with the keys to open the compartment. I was hoping she'd be okay with the five hundred, wouldn't want to do anything else tonight.

In a few moments, she stood out of the car and slammed the door—hard. She thumbed through the bills and her features softened just a little.

"Not bad," she said, finally. She shoved the bills down into one of her back pockets.

"I told you," I said. "And I drove my ass all the way up there. Glad it wasn't a total loss."

"No," she said, stepping closer to me. I tightened up for whatever might happen. She kissed me on the cheek. "My hero. Sort of."

Mody had been quiet this whole time. I felt him pull when Gina was close to us, but I twisted his wrist to keep him with me.

"No, you don't," I told him. "And Ted helped me find this guy, too. Turns out everybody on the island knows him."

I felt the warmth of her hand lingering on my biceps.

"Who is he?"

"They call him Sneakers," I said. "That, Eminem, or M&Ms. Guy's got a lot of nicknames."

Now she smiled, and I knew I was going to be in some trouble. "This is Sneakers?" she asked. "Oh, my God. How'd you manage to get your hands on him? This guy's notorious all over the island."

Mody started to object, but I quieted him with another twist. She said, "He got forty grand out of the Koloas."

"The Koloas? You know them, too?"

"They're meth cooks, mostly, but loan sharks, too. What else they going to do with their money on this island?"

"There's meth here? *Those guys?*"

"What else do regulars do on an island? Shit. It's ugly. But this guy's a local legend. He tell you about his Jordans?"

"He told me."

"They're ones from Malta or something. Historical ones. They're worth like hundreds of thousands of dollars. But that's a myth, right?"

Now Mody was smiling wider than I'd seen before. "They're real."

Gina stepped back. She gave him a long checking over. "Prove it."

"I can. Just tell Jack to take us for a ride, and I'll show you. I can show you both."

She squinted in the light of the parking lot overhead, reading him, looking into his liar's soul. Then her face started to warm up—to him, to whatever she was seeing: truth, desperation, even curiosity of her own, the myth of a legend, or even just a grab for more cash.

Truth was, I was damned curious myself.

We were going for a ride.

19

Going for a Ride

Is it worth explaining how she convinced me? How they both talked me into going for a ride—the three of us? Never mind that I'd been drinking and didn't want to spend any more time driving around that little island; never mind that I just wanted to go back up to the room, tie up Mody, and go to bed; never mind my own curiosity about these Jordans, Mody's bullshit, the Koloa Brothers or whatever other directions I was being pulled in.

Even with the Air Max 95s, the Barkleys and the Jordan Elevens back in my room in San Francisco, I wanted to know. I had to see if the story about this particular pair was true. Mody's tale had hooked me like a fish, and that hook was in deep—all the way down to my gills.

I had to see for myself the pair of sneakers that would make Mody give up all he'd been willing to let go of in their pursuit. I had to see what was at the end of this story.

As Mody pulled my Jeep out of the Sheraton's lot, I asked him, "Where to?" He was driving, with Gina in front beside him. I sat in back in case I needed to do anything drastic. I hoped I wouldn't.

"Where else?" he asked. "We go to the Koloas' place. You said you wanted to get the Jordans back, right?"

"What?"

He laughed. "Just kidding, Jack. Why would the Koloas have them? No, no. We're heading back to my house out past Kekaha."

Gina said, "Oh, I love that beach."

I said, "The fuck? They were at your place this whole time?"

"I mean—" He left it at that and drove on, turned left out on the main road, heading toward the Na Pali coast. Gina didn't seem to mind.

What had lured her to come along? I didn't know. Maybe she had re-warmed to my charms after getting some payback from my Hanalei Bay errand to the Bar Acuda. Maybe she thought there'd be a share of the legend in store for her. Or maybe she too just wanted to see them, to know more about the shoes. I didn't blame her, and definitely didn't mind her being around.

I was also a little leery of where her mood might take her next.

"What's up with the Koloas? Why they looking for the Jordans and you?"

"They— Well, it's a long story."

"I've got time."

Mody had to yell to be heard above the wind. I still had both pieces of the Jeep's top stored in its back. It was getting cold, but I liked the fresh air, the dark night sky above us.

Mody turned his head as he started to explain. "I kind of sold them the Jordans. We were partners in their acquisition, you could say. Look at it like that or like I borrowed their money. I meant to pay them back but with the vig, the figures got away from me."

"So you stole from your firm in San Francisco. Then skipped town."

He caught my eyes in the rear-view, nodded with a heavy measure of shame.

Gina turned around to face me, gave me a special smile. I felt like things were starting to click into place for her, in a way she liked, but I'd already made a habit of reading her wrong. I had that knack with women. It was more than a skill.

She brushed her hand over my knee. "Yeah, about why you're here, Jack. What's your business?"

"His bail bond. Guy who holds it sent me. Now I'm a failed actor *and* a bounty hunter."

"Oh." She winced, but kind of sexy-like. "I think I like that."

"Fucking Leonardi," Mody said. "I should've just paid him off, *then* skipped town."

"But that's how a bond works, M&Ms. He puts up the money because you don't have it. If you had it, you wouldn't have stolen from your firm. And now that you did, you, sir, are wanted. So I'm here to collect you."

He grunted.

"Tell me again why you came out here, back to Kauai?"

"Had to get my Jordans, brother. No point to any of this if I couldn't pay off the K brothers and get my J's back to the mainland."

We passed through a small row of stores, not more than thirty seconds' worth. I missed the sign for the town's name, if it had one. Gina's hand was still on my knee.

"Koloa brothers been holding the Maltese as collateral. Fuck that. They mine. So I come back to pay them off, they wanted more, too much vig, same old song." He spit into the night, out the side of the Jeep. "So I took the Jordans and skipped. Until you came looking."

"What do you mean, 'took the Jordans?'"

"I paid them what I had. Put down the money I stole and left it at that. But they still want the rest of their nut."

Mody drove on. We hit a rough patch, a long series of bumps that jostled us all. Maybe Mody was doing it on purpose.

I said, "Just to be clear: you bought the Jordans with the Koloas' money?"

"Had to." The three of us were quiet then, in the night. Finally, he said, "The Koloas got it like that," as if that explained everything. Perhaps it did.

"Nice collection you left behind though," I said, "in Tiburon."

"You were there? Shit, that was nothing. Those are all retros, re-releases from the past few years. Like two grand for the whole batch."

"Retros? I thought those were the old original pairs."

He caught my eye in the mirror again, realizing I knew a little about the old sneaker game, though not much more. "No, Jack. You see the soles, any yellowing there? No, sir. These days Nike puts those models out almost all the time. Every Saturday a new pair of Jordan Retros drops. Long as you're willing to wait on them."

"I thought— Wait, I thought those were all from back when we were young. They still sell those?"

"No, not like—" He turned around a bit, hit a pot hole, and we bumped hard enough for my ass to leave the seat. I didn't have the gun stuck in the back of Mody's head, which was lucky. Bump like that, my finger could squeeze the trigger. And then where would I be?

"The hot ones sell out in a minute. Stores set up raffles and people cop 'em online in a minute after they release. You get like five windows open on your computer trying to cop. Crazy moments. And it's is a fucking pain here in Hawaii because the release pinned to ten a.m. Saturday morning, East Coast time. That's four a.m. here. You like waking up at 3:30 in the morning to cop your kicks?"

I didn't answer, barely understood what he meant.

"Even in SF, I be setting my alarm for 6:45 to try for them."

"I used to want Jordans in high school," I said. "College even. But I never bought them. Either I couldn't afford them, or they didn't feel right. Not my style or something. Now I wish I had."

"What I'm saying, Jack. You can. The styles are all back again. Not the actual kicks, but Nike remaking anything whenever it wants. Their Retros, OGs, new colorways, anything they can think of. Kids all buy them up more than Kobes, LeBrons, KDs, Kyries and Steph Currys combined!"

Gina looked at me. She pointed out toward the ocean. Now we'd left the towns and I could see palm trees out to our left, beach and open ocean beyond. "When are you two going to quit talking about tennis shoes?"

"Sneakers," I said.

"Nobody talking about tennis, here, sweetheart." Mody waved a finger. "These just kicks, baby. No Lendls, no Stan Smiths, no Andre Agassi joints."

"With the perforated Rod Lavers."

We came to the end of the paved road, and Mody turned off onto dirt, then sand. We got stuck for a few moments, then he shifted to four-wheel, and we kept going. I flashed back to my chase out here with Mody and Mack, wanted to clock him in the head for some retribution.

"Let me ask you," I said. "Once you got out here with the Maltese, what was your next move?"

He scowled at me. "Man, that's what I was figuring out. Then you come fuck things up."

I looked away, turned to Gina. "You ever get out this far?"

She shook her head.

When we could see the house, I caught sight of the other Jeep, Mody's rental, the one I had left with Mack.

"The fuck is he doing here? You and him roommates now?"

Mody swore, but not casually. He put his whole body into it, shoulders and all.

The house was dark, even the porch lights were off. It pissed me off that Mack had found the keys to the Jeep in the brush, rescued himself from the scene outside Mody's mother's.

"Motherfuck." Mody pulled up over the berm and into the driveway, parked the Jeep hard, like a Jeep wants to be parked, and gave the emergency brake a yank. It groaned.

Before he could jump out, I caught his shoulder with one hand, gripped his arm just above the elbow with the other. "You walk with me," I said. "We move together."

He turned to look at my hand, then at my face. "I hear you, man. But if that motherfucker's not there, if I don't find my Jordans... Man! I will shit up in here."

"Okay," I said. "Go look. But we're not partners here.

Leonardi is my partner." I squeezed his arm tighter. "Don't forget. We have a flight to catch in less than eight hours."

"Fuck," he said. "I hear you. Let me go look." I let go of his arm, and he charged out of the Jeep.

Gina watched me. I shrugged. If nothing else, I was learning that Mody had a mind of his own—one that could cook up some fascinating details, at the very least.

"After you?"

She got out of the Jeep in her own time. I wondered what Mody would find inside, whether Mack was waiting for him. I knew I should be on my guard around those two, but I let it slide. Maybe the scotch was having its effect on me, or maybe I was just tired. I wasn't at my best.

Gina turned to me. "You know, you might not be all that bad," she said. "Maybe I misjudged you."

"The first time, or the second?" I asked. When she didn't answer, I slid across the back seat and got out on her side.

She moved closer, and I could feel the pull of her hips drawing mine to her. "I want you, Jack."

That did it for me, broke whatever I had left of my resolve. Her eyebrows came together and she started to say something else, but I cut her off.

"We shouldn't leave him in there long." It was all I could do to keep us both upright.

She leaned in and kissed me lightly on the lips. I was about to return the favor, but then we heard Mody swearing loud from inside. I rushed around the car and up the stairs. There I found the screen door broken off its hinges and left leaning up against the railing. Not a good sign.

The interior door had been kicked out of its frame. Mack couldn't have done that. No, this was more like something the Koloa Brothers would leave behind.

I stepped over the threshold into the living room, called out Mody's name. Gina's heels clacked up the stairs behind me.

"In here." Mody's voice came from down the first hall, in the bedroom.

Then it struck me: no dog noises here. None whatsoever. Where was that yappy terrier?

I flashed back to Ralph's Labrador in El Cerrito, worried I'd have to look at another dog murder, but hoping I wouldn't. Dead dogs were the kind of thing that stuck with you, popped up for months or years in your dreams. Their only advantage, the only use I could see for these mental images, was to put off reaching climax during sex. Imagining a gut-shot Rottweiler could do more to help the female orgasm than French Ticklers, fancy online gadgets, and little blue pills put together.

But that's beside the point.

At the end of the hall, I found Mody descending a ladder from the upstairs loft.

"They're gone!" he said. "The fucking Jordans are missing."

20

Sleepover

"Which Jordans?" I probably shouldn't have asked, didn't need to, but it's what came out of my mouth.

"The fucking Maltese," Mody snapped, like this made him even madder. "The Saudi Elevens. Whatever you want to call them. Jesus! What's the matter with you?"

"Yeah, are you sure—"

"I'm fucking sure. Trust me. And Mack's the only one who knew where I hid them."

I called Mack's name but got back only echoes. "He here?"

Mody said, "No. Fucking no."

"But the car—"

Gina came in behind me. "What's happening?"

While Mody explained, I did a once-through in the kitchen and the other bedroom. I checked both bathrooms too, including behind the shower curtains. All of the closets. Mack wasn't around.

"What's downstairs? Is he down there?"

Mody got madder still. "It's a storage room. Full of shit. I'm the only one who has a key."

I wanted to ask him why he hadn't hidden the Jordans there.

"I told him where the Jordans were in case he had to retrieve them. Maybe even sell them for me if I got put in jail or something. Who the fuck knows what's going to happen with some shit like this?"

"But he drove here. If he's not here now, how'd he get away?"

Gina said, "That's his Jeep?"

"Mine." Mody looked like he wanted to spit. "It doesn't matter. Yeah, I have no idea how he got gone. Unless..." He closed his eyes and pinched the bridge of his nose. "Unless the Koloas followed him here. Then *they* took him away."

It sounded like a decent bet, but I didn't like jumping to conclusions, definitely not ones that featured the Koloas holding everyone's most prized possession. "Call him," I said. "See if he picks up." I handed Mody his phone.

He tapped the screen a few times and then held the phone to his ear. As soon as he did, we heard ringing coming from the kitchen. Gina went over, held up a black iPhone that had been sitting on the counter. I recognized it from when Mack shot of pic of us that morning at his shop, a time that seemed like so long ago.

"Guess he doesn't have his phone on him."

Mody shook his head and swore. "Koloas," he said. "Nobody else would've done this."

"The *fucking* Koloas." I said it more to humor him than out of anger. Whoever these heavyweight bozos tended to think they were, I wasn't intimidated. They'd gotten the better of me once, and I was up for another spin on that wheel.

Gina did her best not to smile. Something in all this struck her as funny.

"They spend their time on the North Shore?"

"No, they're in Kapa'a, by the airport."

I checked my phone for the time. It was after two a.m. and our flight was supposed to leave in six hours. We weren't going to be on it. That much I knew. I'd rebook. Enough was enough for one day and one night of adventure. Plus the extra three hours back to California time put my body at five a.m.

"Let's get some rest. Go after them in the morning." I looked at Gina, and she seemed to be game.

Mody let out a big sigh. "Fuckers," he said. "Yeah. Whatever. You're calling the shots."

I said, "Listen. We'll get your shoes back. The Maltese."

"The Saudi Arabians."

"Whatever. The money ones. I'll put off getting on that plane. We fly out this afternoon, tomorrow, whatever. The bondsman will understand. Or if not, we can cut him in on a piece of the prize."

But Leonardi wouldn't understand. I knew that much. And I had my limits. No way was I ready to drive back across the island to fuck with a Kauaiian mini-gang of extra-large meth-cooking brothers this late at night, even if I could run off to get on a plane back to the mainland right after. I had visions of them following us through security or pulling us out of the line to declare agricultural products at Lihu'e and didn't want any of that.

I didn't like the idea of going straight to the airport, either. Something here had its hook in me; I was not going to walk away now. The wheels of justice would get their man; Leonardi would get his, and I'd get mine. But a mystery like this—about Michael

Jordan and one-of-a-kind, game-worn sneakers? That kind of thing did not come along more than once in a man's life.

"Let's crash out for a while and go after them first thing. Or maybe after breakfast."

"Shit, Jack."

"Take a shower," I said. "Chill the fuck out. Don't do anything crazy. Hear?"

His mood was another reason to pack it in for a while: this angry, he'd be liable to run us into something blind, without thinking clearly. We needed cool heads, a plan, and maybe I was curious about how much Gina had forgiven me.

I held out my hand to Mody. "The phone," I said. "Give it up."

He shrugged, like maybe he'd just forgotten, though I knew he hadn't. Then he pulled it out from a back pocket and handed it over.

"Thanks. And don't think about going anywhere. If I have to tie you up tonight, it's not going to be pretty."

I led Gina down the hall to the first bedroom, the one with the loft entrance.

I heard Mody banging around in the kitchen: running water, opening and closing the refrigerator, knocking things around.

In the bedroom, Gina pushed me down on the bed. "How you feeling, cowboy?" She climbed on and straddled me. We kissed and I started to get in the mood for some activity. Then she stood and walked out.

"Where you going?"

She poked her head in the door. "Cool down a minute while I use the loo."

I pulled myself up to lay my head on the pillow.

The next thing I knew, sun was coming in through the blinds.

I sat up, found Gina's arm across my chest, her topless body next to me, wearing just a pair of black panties. She faced down, her arm and one leg sprawled across me.

I couldn't believe how hard I had slept. The first thing I did was check for my car keys in my pocket, wanting to make sure I hadn't been roofied.

They were still there.

I shook my way out from under Gina, got up and went to the window. Both Jeeps were still in the driveway. The clock read just after eight a.m.

I stumbled down the hall, relieved myself and splashed water on my face. I walked into the kitchen, got a glass and poured myself some cold water from the tap. I drank long and hard, poured another glass and did it again. The water tasted so damned good, probably piped down from the island mountain. A pleasure of paradise.

Mody was in his room, sitting up on the bed when I walked in.

He asked me, "You have yourself a good night?"

"I've had better. Did you sleep at all?"

He shook his head. "Thinking about how we get back those kicks."

"Get any ideas?"

He stood up. "You know I did."

21

Partners?

Mody made us strong coffee using island beans that were only sold to locals. He explained with pride about the island coffee crop, the proprietary way local farmers protected their best beans for the native islanders, and how Montsanto and other big corporations were elbowing their way into the heart of all agriculture, pushing the islanders to get even more defensive.

"It's like us versus them," he said. He poured me a mug and pushed it across the counter. "Try this."

I liked my coffee light and sweet—like my ladies—but didn't make the point. I lifted the mug and inhaled, got a good sense of the aroma and the flavors, then tasted it. It had all I could expect from Island Paradise Productions, enough that I only took a little cream. Turned out he drank his the same way.

"So what's the deal with the girl?" he asked. "I'm not cutting her in on this."

I started to say something, then stopped. My thinking was something between not knowing her angle and wanting to get her the rest of the money she needed to leave the island. If it came down to it, I would carve it out of my own cut—if any of this panned out.

"Let me worry about her."

Maybe it was naïve to imagine Gina happy with her money from the bar, but I didn't stop to consider it. If these sneakers led to a payday, I wouldn't mind handing some of it to Gina. It was basically found money to me, anyway.

Mody took a long drink of coffee and then stared across the counter. "So what's your angle, Jack? What's it going to take?"

"Who, me?" I smiled, but Mody didn't crack. So I went right to the truth. "First, we're going back to collect that bond. Don't expect that to disappear. Second, you have to make this worth my while. I don't see that coming in for anything less than half."

"*Half?*"

If what Mody said was true about these Jordans, if they were that rare, then maybe he could sell them for… what? I had no idea the worth of something like that. Who did? One hundred thousand? Two? Maybe even more.

Whatever it was, I could live with getting back double my money and more on top of Leonardi's paycheck. No question. And for what? Just my investment of a day or two extra on the island. What could that hurt?

Mody pursed his lips, waiting me out.

"Half," I said.

"I hear you. Let's just be sure we get them first, then we figure out your cut."

So I pressed him: I started around the counter in the kitchen, backed him against the sink and started to crack my knuckles. "Come on, man. We decide this now and here, or we go right to the airport."

"Okay," he said. "Deal. What you don't understand is that this is a part of history, man. It's not just about money. Nothing is ever just money. These are a basketball and cultural relic. Don't you understand that?"

I held up my hands in surrender. "No doubt about it. We need to get these back into the right hands. These need to be preserved for antiquity. But also we sell them."

"To the right person. The right collector."

"Absolutely."

"What are you two discussing in here?" Gina walked in from the bedroom, dressed in her clothes from last night but looking as fresh as the first time I'd met her. She went right for the coffee, smelled it, and smiled. Mody beamed. She was a sight to behold, even first thing in the day, enough to make me forget the green mountains and lush palm trees outside the windows.

Gina found a mug in the cabinet, went back to the pot, and then poured her coffee. When she turned to us to get the cream and sugar, I think we both did our best to act uninterested, but she just laughed.

"Good morning, boys. How did you two sleep?" Then she winked at me.

I started to answer, but she was already heading out to the porch to admire the scenery. Over her shoulder, she asked about our plan: if we had one, and if so what it was.

"We find Mack and the Koloas," Mody said. "Get the kicks back and jet out. Whatever it takes, then get to wherever the brothers are not."

She was quiet for a time on the porch. Mody had given me a more detailed plan of attack before making coffee, but it basically boiled down to that: breaking and entering, a snatch and grab. So be it.

I drank a few glasses of water and did a few stretches to loosen up. Then I hit the shower fast, taking the car keys with me. I told Mody not to try any shit.

"Come on, man. We're partners now, right?"

"Nope. We may be partners in money when the pay comes, but you're still my prisoner, like it or not."

He didn't. But I didn't care.

22

Money

When I stepped out of the shower, my phone was ringing: Leonardi. I wrapped a towel around my waist and answered.

"Tell me you're at the airport, Jack, about to get on a plane."

I knew if I lied it'd give me a couple hours of leeway before he found the truth, but that it would piss him off more once he did. So I told him the truth: "Good news, bad news, Joe. Good is I have Mody. Bad is we're not taking that first flight out. We got hung up. Still, I'll have him home soon."

I could hear his teeth grinding through the phone. "What is that? Hung up? I don't trade in vague bullshit, Jack. There's more to this now. New forces coming into play. Give me something solid, something real."

"Just clearing up a debt he has on the island. Trust me, Joe. We do this now, *then* we come back. It's all for the better. Otherwise it seeks us out and bites us in the ass."

I studied my face in the mirror, wondering how this version of me speaking these lines would look on the big screen.

"Paint me a picture, Jack. Put details in it. Because I have some dark ones for you."

"It's more with the shoes. Turns out some island fat-cat

wannabes banked Mody to a stake of some Michael Jordan memorabilia we need to get clear of. It's something really serious from Jordan's secret closet. Worth big dough."

A sound came through the phone then. It might've been a dog at Leonardi's house or him laughing at what I'd just said. As far as I knew, he didn't own a dog.

"You're telling me sneakers, Jack? Do I have this right? Fucking pair of sneakers?"

I said, "We have to do this for the good of NBA history, Joe. These things, they can't wind up in the wrong hands."

"Fuck me, Jack. Say that again. Say the part about history."

"I said, it's for the good of—"

"Fuck *you*, Jack! Do you know how stupid that sounds? You think I give a shit about basketball history, Jack? This is about money. M. O. N. E."

"I—"

"Let me give you a piece of reality that contradicts this shit you're spinning. North Beach. The family there. Do you know it?"

"But this is Jordan—"

"Italians, Jack. *The Family.* As in *the* only family that matters. Right? These are the people who backed Mody's accounting firm. They're the ones he stole from. Do you hear this?"

"Yeah. I hear you." *Family* came through loud and clear.

"Hear me now, Jack. Get this bitch home so I get my money. That's it. Period. Get his ass back in jail."

"Okay, Joe."

"Say you hear me."

"I hear you."

"Otherwise I get Mahogany. And we both know you don't want that. It's Mahogany first and behind that the people from North Beach. So it's done now. Over."

I gave him my agreement, but by that time he had already hung up. Mahogany was a name I knew, one of SF's bigger hunters. If Leonardi was bringing her up now, it meant she had turned him down earlier, and maybe now she was free. She would always be a first choice to somebody like Joe Leonardi, preferable to me. She was a professional. Basically a corporation. Me? Even I wasn't quite sure what I was.

And if Mahogany flew out to the island, it wasn't good for me—financially or otherwise. In short, that was a version of events I did not want to see.

I walked out of the bathroom to find Mody ogling Gina's ass as she cooked up some eggs.

"Well," I said. "Word from on high is we get this done fast and I get you back today."

Mody agreed. "Right after we get the kicks."

"Take your food to go."

Gina shuffled scrambled eggs onto a plate for herself and started eating. Mody served himself from what was left. Bad news was, he didn't leave any for me.

"No more?" I said. Then I took the plate out of his hands and started in on it. "Guess you'll have to pick something up."

"That's cold, Jack. You know that's not right."

With my mouth full, I said, "Tell it to the Koloas. Ask them to make you some breakfast. Or we'll get you some pretzels on the plane."

23

You're Jack Palms, Man

I drove this time. Mody sat next to me in the front, Gina in the back. Without punctured tires, driving on the sand was fun again: the combination of wrestling the Jeep into control, driving in tracks that had already been created, and cruising right along the ocean, even dipping the wheels into the surf once or twice.

By the time we were back near the Sheraton, Gina had made it clear she was done with this ride. Whatever we were heading into next was going to be less fun and more work or danger. In short, she'd heard enough about the Koloas to want to keep her distance, and I didn't argue.

We pulled into the hotel turnaround to drop her off, and I got out to have a few words.

"Give me a minute," I told Mody and took the keys.

I held Gina's hand as we walked toward the entrance of the hotel, feeling lucky that the bellhops and valets weren't around this early in the a.m. The guys here now were older and didn't seem to know Gina; their shifts likely never overlapped.

"Listen, no matter what happens here today, I'm going to need to get on a plane back to San Francisco right after." I didn't know what to say beyond this. So far, we hadn't had the best of communication. Maybe my best tack was to let her down easy and glide out while I still could.

"I know," she said. "But I'm out of here, too. My time's up on this rock. Maybe I'll see you back stateside sometime. You owe me a drink after last night. *At least.*"

She winked at me and was gone, walked off into the lobby to go back to her island life—or whatever was left of it. Nest egg, back tips, or just a handful of bills collected from Ted. She seemed glad about that. And she'd gotten the last line on me here, but I had a feeling I'd be seeing her again sooner or later.

I climbed back into the Jeep with Mody, gunned the engine, and peeled us out of the hotel. We tore up the pavement back to the main road and from there we cruised around the southeast corner of the island, past the airport and up toward Kapa'a in the middle of the eastern coast.

The Koloas lived on a road that turned off from the highway and headed away from the beach. Instead of heading up into the hills and mountains, this road and the whole area around it kept right along in the flats. Off in the distance, we could see dark green mountains under a wide, clear sky. Grass ran along both sides of the narrow road, a strip of unbroken blacktop that offered no lines—white, yellow, or dotted. The houses sat back from the road just a little, behind low walls and rows of trees: palms mostly, but also plenty of shrubs I didn't know anything about.

Finally, Mody said to slow down, that it was coming up. He had me pull over on the left, onto an empty patch of grass across from a low, one-story house just like all the others. A familiar big pickup and a black SUV were parked in the drive.

"This is them," he said.

"They all live together? The guys you've got a problem with? They're all related *and* still live together?"

He shrugged. "Family is very important here. Plus, they've got a little add-on in the back beyond what you see. This place bigger than it looks."

"You used to be friends with them?"

"Yeah. You might say." He sat in his seat, not moving, instead only staring at the house. "But no one is ever really friends with the Koloas."

I cut the engine. Though it wasn't yet nine thirty, the sun beat down on us and the air was hot.

"These guys back in SF, they're *really* not your friends. Okay? We get this done and get you back to settle with them. Either you're behind bars, or it's open season on you. Get me?"

He nodded. "Think Mack's in there?" he asked.

"I thought you were only worried about your shoes."

"Mostly. But he's a friend."

I pulled myself out of the Jeep and hopped down onto the grass, kicked out my legs to get ready—to run or to fight, either way.

"They usually have other cars here? Or is this it?"

The night before I'd dealt with three of them, which wasn't as bad as it could've been. Now I needed to know how many to expect.

"These and sometimes a sedan. There's four brothers, plus their mother lives here. Her ride was a sedan, so I'm guessing she's out."

"Good. We've dealt with moms enough already." I stopped,

struck by an idea I should've thought of earlier. "Are your mothers in contact with one another? Can we just have them work it out, matriarch-style, and get the sneakers back?"

Mody turned, looked at me like I was an idiot. "This ain't junior high, Jack. Even if it is about some sneakers. Despite what you might be thinking, this shit is for real. Not something we can just fuck around with, get somebody's mom to take care of."

"All right," I said. "Fine. What are their names? Let me get that clear, at least."

Mody said, "Their mom has a thing for *The Tonight Show*. Freaking loves it. Named them after Carson, McMahon, Severinson, and Leno."

"You're shitting me."

He raised a hand. "Honest to Jesus."

"Fine."

I started around the back of the Jeep, stopped on the grass, and looked both ways up and down the street. Mody waited for my next move.

"Wait." I went back to my seat, leaned in, got the gun out from underneath it. One thing I was learning: it was better to have a gun and not need it than the other way around.

"Good," he said, looking toward the house. "You're likely to need that."

I shook my head, still unsure what a mess I was getting into. "What haven't you told me? What am I walking into here?"

Mody paused before answering, like he didn't want me to think about it. "Best guess? They're just waking up and we come in, catch them off guard, get what we're looking for."

"Yeah. Sounds too easy."

He shrugged. "Maybe it is. Or maybe we catch them finishing up a fresh batch of meth, using or cooking, either way, and they're geared up to grind us up into sawdust. But shit, what are the odds of that?"

"That's what I'm asking."

"You? You're Jack Palms, man. Shit. You got this!"

I didn't trust him, no didn't like where this was going one bit, but I trusted myself to get back out of it if things went south—with Mody in tow. So the clock was ticking, flights were leaving, and I had one shot at the sneakers.

I was going to take it.

24

Wake 'Em Up

I pounded on the front door with the butt of the gun. Maybe the direct approach wasn't always best, but I was running short on time. If we could make the next flight to the mainland, I might avoid the Mahogany scenario altogether.

"Open up. We know you're in there." I sounded like a cop and didn't like that, but what could I do? Sometimes you sound like a cop. It's part of the job.

A woman's voice responded through the door. She sounded like somebody's mother. "Who *is* it?"

"I'm looking for the brothers. Your sons, ma'am."

"What's your name?"

"I'm Albert Culpepper."

"Bull. Shit. I can see your face."

I checked the peep hole. Sure enough, right in front of me.

"And is that M&Ms standing there with you? What's he doing back on island?"

The door opened. Before me stood a woman who came up to my chest and almost filled the doorframe sideways. Squat didn't begin to describe her.

"That's Jack Palms, ain't you?" She pointed at my face and

smiled, kind of did a winking thing that might've looked sexy on a woman thirty years younger and half her weight.

"Ma'am?" I was trying to play it as polite as possible.

"Don't bullshit me, boy. You from the movies. I *know* you."

I gave in and agreed, shrugged, made sure not to show her the gun. Instead I tucked it down the back of my shorts and made sure my shirt hung over it.

She smiled into a full blush, stepped back and invited us in. "How you been, Meyer?" she asked.

I shot him a look and held the door open. He went in.

"I'm good. Things been fine. Are the boys awake yet?"

"No, no. They're still sleep. Why don't you two come in, have some coffee, and I'll wake them."

"Not necessary, Momma Koloa. Not at all. Is Malcolm here? From the surf shop out Poipu?"

"Somebody came in with them late, but I was sleep. Sit. Sit!" She steered Mody toward a plastic-covered couch, complete with doilies on the arms. He sat. I didn't. "Can I get you two some coffeecake? Mr. Palms?"

"No thanks, ma'am."

"It really *is* you, isn't it? I saw you in that movie, you know. Which one was it?"

A few moments passed as she thought. Mody asked for some of the coffeecake.

"You be quiet, now. What was the name of his picture? Comes on cable all the time still."

Mody finally caught on. It was a slow burn, to say the least. "You know this guy?" he asked her.

"He's an *actor*, is what I've been saying." She slapped him on

131

the knee, turned to me. "What was the name of that movie? Tell us."

"*Shake 'Em Down.*" I didn't say it any specific way, just said it like a fact, the same as any other. Like a day of the week or what month it was.

"That's right!" Her voice went up an octave. She stepped back.

Mody turned to get a better look at me, hamming it up to go along. "I saw that one." He raised his eyebrows like it was a big deal. "That was *you*?"

I nodded. "Fuck you. And it was."

"Say that thing!" she said.

Mody chimed in, "That thing! Say it!"

"He knows. Say the thing!" She pointed at me.

I said what she wanted to hear, said it just as seriously as I had in the movie: "You took my city. Now I want it back."

"Ha!" She laughed and pointed at me like I'd hit it exactly. I had practice times a thousand by now. Maybe more. "Yeah! Yeah. Now say the other thing."

This was how it always went: no one ever satisfied once I started down this road.

Behind her, the biggest brother I'd seen the other night, the one called Doc, waddled in wearing a baggy tank top and basketball shorts, looking half-asleep. "What's happening?" he asked.

"This movie man come to see you boys about something with Meyer here. Don't you recognize him?"

This one knew who I was, remembered how I'd lit him up with a right hook and an uppercut. Maybe he'd save me from his mom's interrogation, but he looked pissed. Like some kind of parlor trick, he produced a toothpick slowly from inside his mouth and started to chew it.

I said, "I just want to talk. A couple minutes."

His eyes narrowed; his jaw clenched. "You owe me something."

His mother turned and yelled at him, "Doc Severinsen Koloa!"

"What's that?" I asked, bristling for the fight again.

He brought his fists up. "Another chance, haole."

"What, boy? This early you start with that? With our guest?"

He crunched through the toothpick, chewed it, and spit fibers on the ground.

"Boy!" she yelled.

He stooped to pick up the pieces. "Okay," he said to me, "out back."

"Fine with me." I walked towards him, waiting to follow his lead.

Mody stood up behind me. "Does this mean I'm not getting coffeecake?"

Momma Koloa said, "There's no fighting in this house, you hear?"

"Yes, ma'am," Doc said.

I walked past him into the kitchen, steering myself toward a back door I didn't yet know existed, when a second brother appeared from behind the refrigerator, with a huge slice of coffeecake in his hand. This was the one who'd tackled me onto Mody's parents.

"What's he doing here?" he asked Doc.

"We got business," I said.

"Damn right we do. You're gonna help us get our money."

"First your brother wants to fight." I thumbed toward Doc, who walked in behind me.

Mody came in, too. "Johnny. Let me get some of that coffeecake."

Doc said, "You don't eat all the cake now."

"Where's Mack?" I asked. "You guys got him here somewhere?"

Johnny stared me down from beside the refrigerator, trying to act hard. "He went to work. We let him. What you really want now?"

Mody sat down at the kitchen table, pulled the coffeecake towards him and lifted out a slice. "You know what we want. My shoes."

"Our shoes." Doc pulled the rest of the coffeecake away from Mody. "*Our* shoes."

Mody took a big bite, shrugged and said something that was supposed to be "my shoes" but through a mouthful of cake it was impossible to understand.

Their mother came into the kitchen. "No fighting, hear? And you all best share that."

Johnny said, "Momma, give us a few minutes, okay?"

She started to protest, then caught the look in her sons' eyes and walked out, headed toward whatever rooms were in the front of the house. "I know, I know," she said, "Business. Always business."

"Go get the others," Johnny said to Doc. "Get them now."

Doc didn't say a word. He handed the cake to his brother, then followed his mother out. I heard him waking the others: calling their names and knocking on doors.

I said, "We want the kicks."

Johnny set the cake pan on top of the refrigerator, then opened the door and removed a plastic milk gallon jug. I saw at least five of them on the shelves, each with a different name on it in marker. He drank right out of his. Twin lines of white dribbled down the sides of his mouth. He gasped when he finished, swore, said, "So what?"

Mody said, "You stole them. We want 'em back."

"So?" Johnny nodded. "Keeping 'em too."

I checked Mody to see how he wanted to proceed. Far as I could tell, he wanted to talk. I didn't. I started toward Johnny, ready to take him outside. "Let's go, beefcake. Mom wants you to take it outside, so let's do it."

Johnny threw the milk jug at my face. I turned away, let it hit my shoulder, but he was right behind it. He piled onto me, and we both went down hard onto the kitchen table. It broke underneath us, the sugar bowl and napkin dispenser sent flying along with a lazy Susan of pill bottles. Chairs scattered.

"Johnny Carson!" Their mother called out from the front of the house, then Doc reappeared by the refrigerator and rushed to pull his brother off me.

"Come on. You heard her. We take this outside."

"Damage done, bro."

They both stood over me, Mody off to the side.

Then Mrs. Koloa was in the kitchen. I stayed down to act the victim, see how she handled it. First she started hitting Johnny Carson around his shoulders and, when he ducked for cover, his head. "What did I tell you? Just now even. You dumbfuck! Dumbshit!"

"Mah," he said. "Leave it be. I'll pay for it."

She hit him again. "No fighting in the house!"

I got my feet under me and backed away, gathering myself by the doorway to the living room, ready for whatever would come next. All of a sudden another one of the brothers came out through a door I hadn't even noticed—a bathroom off the kitchen. He was pulling up his pants and then charged at me with as much speed and momentum as he could muster. I did my best to dodge, just managed to get out of the way and helped him crash into the archway entry for the living room. The collision shook the whole house. Plaster fell from the ceiling.

"Eddie!" their mother yelled. "What is *wrong* with you?"

Now big Eddie stood up straight. I backed off, making my way into the living room. He pushed off the wall just below where he'd left a dent, and came at me again. I used whatever I could gather in the way of misdirection to throw him into the living room, onto what turned out to be a crushed coffee table as soon as he hit it.

"Fuck! Eddie!" Momma Koloa howled.

I felt another brother behind me: Doc grabbed my arms, held them to my body. I didn't want to see what Momma would do next if we broke anything else. This getting bad, but somewhere in the house they had the shoes we needed.

"Hold up, Jacky boy," a new voice said, this one higher-pitched and more reasoned than the rest. "Just you keep still."

25

Red Harvest

Now Doc turned me around, and I saw the fourth brother enter the room, the one I hadn't seen at Mody's. He was smaller than the others and younger by a few years. This would be the one named after Jay Leno. If they all had the same mother, he came from a different father for sure—looked like maybe a white guy from the mainland, which I was sure would cause strife. He pulled Mody in behind him, cradling his neck in a choke hold, and yanking him around.

I could hear Johnny walking their mother toward the bedrooms, doing his best to calm her down.

"I'm not moving," I said. Even if I wanted to, Doc held me tight.

Big Eddie got up off the floor behind us. To the smaller brother, he said, "I got this, Jay. Hang on." He came around to look me in the face. "I should break you right now," he said.

Mody said, "Do what they tell you, Jack."

Doc told his brother where I had a gun, and Eddie went for it. He plucked it right out of the back of my shorts.

"This," he said. "You brought *this* into our house?" Eddie shook his head. "That is *terrible* manners." Then he cracked me across the cheek with its stock while his brother held me still.

I tasted blood on the inside of my mouth and spit onto the floor. Let my biggest fan clean that up once her boys had finished with me.

Even Mody said, "Jesus, Jack."

I laughed. This whole thing was becoming a comedy of errors. A series of mistakes that was drawing me deeper and deeper into trouble.

Eddie paced in front of me, waiting to decide his next move, but Leno whistled to get his attention, then stopped him in his tracks with one look.

"Bring it," I said. "Show me what you got, boys."

Instead Leno tightened his grip on Mody's neck, putting on the full squeeze. Mody whined. His knees buckled. Leno said, "Take him outside."

Doc walked me backward toward the front door. Eddie went around to open it, and we all walked outside onto the welcome matt.

I heard Mody scream from back in the living room, and I pictured Johnny and Leno working him over, trying to find out where he had his money. Eddie slammed the door shut behind him. Now it was just the three of us outside: me, Doc and Eddie. Doc let me go, which almost made it a fair fight, except Eddie was holding a gun.

The funny part was that I knew it wasn't loaded, that I'd left the bullets back in the glove box of my Jeep, and I was the only one. Eddie didn't seem eager to use it as anything other than a blunt object anyway.

He spread his arms. "We out here now, Jack. What you want,

really? What you come to this island for?"

"Mody," I said. "I'm taking him back."

"So why you come here then? You had him." He shook his big head slowly. "Uh uh. Try again."

"Mody and now the shoes."

He smiled as wide as his face could handle. "The Maltese Jordans," he said. Then he laughed. "They legend. You for real think they exist? And we let you just walk away with them?"

I shifted my weight from one foot to another, waiting for one of them to make a move. I also read his face, trying to read any tell he might be giving up. Nothing.

"Well are they?"

His face barely moved as he said, "Oh, they real. And they here. Where they gonna stay."

"Let me see them."

Now his smile widened as he nodded. Suddenly he understood what I was doing. Maybe I did too. "You look, you leave?"

"What about Mody?"

"You take him back dead, does that help you?"

I thought it over: how I'd get a dead man onto a plane, what Joe Leonardi would say about that, and whether I thought they'd actually kill him. I didn't have good answers to any of these, except about me getting a dead man onto a plane. I didn't want any *Weekend at Bernie's* shenanigans. And I knew I'd be screwed if I went back without him. So my only choice was to press on.

"No. I need him alive. Let's work this out." That took things down about seven levels. They looked like they still didn't trust me, but it went from an eleven to about a four.

We all walked back inside, where we found Mody massaging his neck, and Momma Koloa reading her boys the riot act.

"What's this all about?" she asked. "You boys all come clean or I go wild for all the damage you done to my furniture."

Leno said, "Jesus. We'll pay for it!"

She slapped him across the back of his head. "The Lord's name!"

"But we—"

She shook her head. "Jack Palms, what going on here?"

"Just some friendly trading gone wrong, I'm afraid. Seems like your boys' friend, Mr. Mody here, borrowed money from your boys to purchase a high-priced item and now they have taken it back."

Mody jumped in. "It's not like I didn't want to pay them back. I just need to sell the kicks first, *then* I'll have the money."

All of the brothers stared holes in his chest.

"*All* your money," Mody said. "But come on, you got to let up on that vig. It's ridiculous!"

"What?" Mrs. Koloa threw her hands up. "You boys going bananas with that vig again? What'd I tell you about that practice."

Eddie lowered his eyes. "Not to run it up too high."

Leno chimed in, "Especially not on locals."

"That's right! No Shylocking true islanders. He's your friend!"

I stepped back. A part of me was about to lose my mind with this, but I also knew it was deadly serious—Mody had stolen a big chunk of change from his San Francisco firm to pay these guys. And now that I knew who was backing this firm, whose money it was, and what kind of goons he was trying to pay off, I was certain he'd robbed the wrong Peter to pay Paul.

"Do you even realize what you've done here? The level of trouble this has caused?"

"All we need to do," Mody said, "is sell the shoes."

"How?"

"Where?"

"New York City. There's a big sneaker convention there this weekend. SneakerCon. People there will know about these shoes. Trust me: they will be a highlight of unbelievable proportions. *That's* where we can make some real cheddar selling these. Then we can *all* get paid."

I didn't have to do any mental math to figure out the pie was getting split into smaller and smaller portions if we went forward with paying off the Koloas, then Mody got his, and I got mine, with Gina's share in there, too. The risks were getting ever higher and the payoff, not so much. Plus with the Italian family from San Francisco involved now, too, it was shaping up to be a big fucking mess. Too big of one to keep my feet in. I was ready to let the Koloas have the shoes, settle that score with Mody for them by any means, and let him go right to jail. I would take my cut from Leonardi, avoid Mahogany and the Italians, and be fully finished. Shoes, Jordans, NBA history, bigger payouts and everything else involved, I was ready to let it go.

"I'm ready to bring this all to an end," I said. "I have a solution that should make everyone happy. Just one thing."

The Koloas nodded. Their mother spoke for them, asked me what my stipulation was.

"I need to see these Jordans. The Maltese."

Mody perked up. "Yeah," he said. "Take us to the shoes."

Mrs. Koloa looked at her sons. They both rolled their eyes.

"These shoes," Leno said, "they are purely the stuff of legend. You probably haven't even seen the YouTube."

"There's a YouTube?" I said.

"So go get 'em," said Momma Koloa.

"Uh uh. You come with us." Leno turned and led us back toward the kitchen. Johnny was hanging out by the refrigerator, eating cake. He looked like he wanted to eat me. I knew all four of them together could take me apart piece by piece and kick Mody's ass up and down the block, but they weren't doing it. Something about their island-gangster sensibility preferred the competition of the one-on-one combat or one-on-two to the gang jump destruction, and I could appreciate that—the chivalry of it all—it was keeping me alive.

Leno waved Johnny aside. "I'm taking him in," he said.

Mody said, "You aren't going to believe these, Jack. Incredible!"

Eddie grabbed Mody from behind and pushed him back into the living room. "You stay out here," he said.

Leno jabbed his index finger into my sternum, smiling like a proud father. "You come."

26

YouTube

They led me back through the kitchen and down the hall to the back rooms. At the last of them, the door was locked. Eddie produced a thick chain from inside his shirt and took it off over his head. A single key hung from it like a pendant.

He unlocked the door and stood aside.

Leno walked into the room, and Doc pushed me from behind to follow.

Inside, the room was bare but for a single shaded window and a futon couch. Leno knelt down at the couch and slid a footlocker out from underneath. Eddie handed him a key that he used to open it.

When the lid came up, I thought for a moment they had lit the thing from the inside. But there were no lightbulbs there, just a single golden shoebox. Light from a high window shone into the room and reflected impossibly off the gold. I almost had to shield my eyes from the glow of it.

"Damn," Leno said, "sure is nice."

Doc and Eddie said the same thing, almost at once. "First, the YouTube."

Leno said, "Yeah. I get it." He took a laptop out of the

footlocker, then closed the lid and set the computer down on top. As soon as the lid closed, the room seemed to dim, like the sun coming in was actually magnified by its reflection off the gold.

"Was that?" I asked. I couldn't tell if the box had been cardboard or something stronger, but it looked nicer than if it were just spray-painted cardboard; I thought it might actually be covered with gold leaf.

"Is that?"

Leno nodded. "Yeah. We couldn't believe it, either. But first this." He fired up the computer and waited a minute for it to boot. The room was a tight little number, just four walls, a high window, and the futon. If this was anybody's bedroom, it hadn't been used in a while.

Leno looked past me to his brothers. "Man, I want to show him. Touch them again."

They both said no. That we all had to wait. "The YouTube," one of them said.

"Okay, okay." Leno started typing into the browser's search bar. He typed a long string of characters that didn't look like words or any URL I recognized. Then I noticed a scrap of yellow sticky note taped to the grey frame above the monitor. "This isn't YouTube," Leno said. "More like dark web. We pulled this from an email Eminem sent us back in his funding proposal stage. This convinced us. And still no idea how that son of a bitch found it, like some sort of sneakerhead dark message board. Who knows?"

A funny-looking search box opened on his screen and Leno typed something with "Jordan" and "Malta" into the field. A pair of grainy videos came up. Behind me, Doc chuckled. "Love this," he said.

Leno shifted his legs so he was kneeling on both knees in front of the locker. "I still can't believe he found this. Who the hell could *do* that?"

He clicked on the first video, and I leaned forward. As the image box expanded, I recognized the grainy footage that everyone used back in the '90s on tape-based camcorders, pre-digital, before HD was even a concept in some nerd's dream. What I saw there looked like some kind of gym, wood floors and stacked wooden bleachers. Almost like a high school. Nobody in the frame—someone was just figuring out the camera. I could hear talking, not in English. Sounded like some kind of Arabic.

Then I heard a deep voice that I thought I recognized as Michael's—that unmistakable baritone, the confidence it exuded.

"Can you turn it up?" I asked.

Leno shook his head. "Nah. That's as loud as it goes. He's not close to the camera. And the equipment, as you can see, is pretty much the basics from that era."

Then the camera moved, panned across the court, and I saw some players I thought I recognized. Alaa Abdelnaby talked to a shorter guy in a yellow jersey. Then I saw someone I knew without a doubt.

"That has to be," I said. I couldn't help myself, I'd come forward, was pointing at the screen.

"Cap," Leno said. "Big Lew, the man himself. Kareem Abdul Jabbar. Dude who fought Bruce Lee in fucking *Game of Death*. Goddamn."

I swore. There was no mistaking the man: arms from here until forever, long legs, shaved head, big goggles perched above his eyes. "Sky hook," I said.

And then the frame shifted and I saw who Kareem was talking to: MJ. Michael Jordan.

The frame bounced, as if someone had bumped into the camera. Jordan left the frame and all I saw was wooden floor again. Staccato exclamations in Arabic, like someone swearing. Then the video cut out. It was over.

"You didn't see them, did you?" Leno looked at me, waiting.

"What? I saw him. But I don't know where the hell that was. Could've been a practice for an All-Star game or something."

"No. No. No. You know what you saw." He started to adjust a slider underneath the video, pulling it back to where Jordan was on the screen. He clicked a few features and then pressed pause and now it started moving forward again, but slowly. This was some sort of super slo-mo version of the footage I'd just seen. The cameraman got bumped. A sound like someone hitting the mic. Then the camera went shaky, even more blurry, and the frame shifted. First it zigged right and Jordan cut out. Then it zagged left, and I saw Jordan again, still next to Kareem.

"Now." Leno lifted his hand and timed a final click of the trackpad carefully. The image froze just as the camera panned down, toward what would eventually just be a shot of the floor. But he had stopped it before that happened. And when he did, there they were, impossibly captured right in the middle of the screen, below the long shorts, the calf-sleeve, and the short socks: a pair of Jordan Elevens with gold where the black patent leather would usually be. I saw them there on his feet, studded with jewels—shiny stones that I couldn't have told you anything about except that they were there. He had them right on his screen.

"That's them," Leno said, "the Maltese," and he basically took the words right out of my mouth, my head even. I knew what I was looking at, and that Mody had absolutely been telling the truth all along.

27

The Box

"What's on the other video?" I asked.

Leno laughed. "That one? Not so much."

Back on the main screen, he clicked the other thumbnail and the window expanded again. This time, more of the grainy footage appeared, now followed by even more staticky images like a basketball game were being played in a gym full of snow— like it was snowing inside the gym. And of course it wasn't. This was Malta or Saudi Arabia, I knew, could recognize the bursts of encouragement in Arabic and the attire: headdresses and robes in what would pass for stands. The camera seemed most interested in these: the stands and spectators, and one in particular with a wide swath of fabric wrapped around his head and shoulders, held in place by what looked to be a black headband.

"That the king?" I asked.

"We're guessing." Leno pointed at the screen. "Here's a glimpse."

On camera I saw a very lanky, dark man cross half court with his dribble. It could have been Mike, but I would not have sworn to it.

Leno stopped the video. "The rest of it goes on like this. I wish I could tell you it had some awesome highlights: MJ on the drive, dunking over Cap or Abdelnaby, but no. Not so much. It's mostly like they wanted to video the king watching the game. He claps. He cheers."

Doc came around. "Like they just wanted their king watching for posterity. Not the game." He held out his big hands. "Who knows? But there it is. Enough to make *me* a believer."

I could hear Mody calling to us from the kitchen: "It's true. I swear it's all true." Then, when I turned, his face was in the doorway. "Show him the sneakers. Or here, let me."

Eddie caught him at the door, held him out, and then pushed him back. He finally shoved Mody out of the room with one big hand. "Johnny," he called, "can you hold this fool?"

Then the door closed and Mody was gone. He yelled, "They're legit! You know it."

We all turned back to Leno, who had closed the laptop and set it on the futon. He held the lid of the footlocker, ready to lift it. "You ready?" he asked me. "You a believer?"

I said, "I believe." I stood on the balls of my feet, wanting to jump, but patiently waiting. I had come this far. "Let's see them."

Then he opened the lid, and I saw the gold again, the glow from within the locker that almost didn't seem possible. Sure, we were in Hawaii, on Kauai, but I didn't think the room was that sunny or that the window let in enough light to make the effect possible. Yet it did. I saw the dust motes in the air, floating in the sun rays and the gleam off the gold box, which magnified as Leno picked it up, lifted it out of the footlocker. I squinted as he did, wishing I had my sunglasses.

He set the sneaker box on the couch and shoved the footlocker back underneath.

In a second, my eyes adjusted to the new light. I could see now that the box was actually two-toned gold. One matte layer for the background, and on the top another for the signature Jordan Jumpman silhouette. There in shiny, polished gold, his legs spread eagle, one hand stretching back, one hand reaching up holding the ball. It reminded me of the dunk contest in 1988, his dunk from the foul line, but I knew the original image couldn't have come from that. It was from a poster I'd seen on my friends' walls in high school. Or a commercial. Nothing he'd ever done in a game.

Leno rapped a knuckle against the top of the box. It had to be some kind of metal. Sure, it couldn't be solid gold, I didn't think, but it was not cardboard.

"Is that…?"

Leno shrugged. "Your guess is good as mine. But it's hard. Solid." He rapped on it again.

"Open the lid." My hands were sweating now. Something about what I was seeing tapped into a part of me still left over from when I was a teenager, back when basketball had been my main religion. My true north.

Leno turned to me then. He laughed under his breath. "Look at him. He's just like us. These fucking things. They capture that part of us all." I watched him rub his palm over the Jumpman logo, wishing I could do the same.

Behind me, Eddie said, "Why we need to just sell 'em. Get 'em out of our lives and move that shit along. Cash it in."

Doc agreed.

"But maybe," Leno said, "this is all we have here. The item, the anticipation, the meeting of myth and reality." His eyes locked on mine. "What do you say, Jack? Would you give something significant to know what's inside?"

I said, "I already have."

Without checking my watch, I knew we'd likely missed another flight back to the mainland, that I was getting closer and closer to the mafia and Mahogany with every passing hour.

"Maybe this is worth more than money," Leno said. "Just having these. Knowing we can see them any time."

Neither of the other brothers spoke. We were all waiting for what came next.

"Just show me," I said.

"Patience, Jack. Patience." Leno pulled out a second shoebox from under the futon, this one just black, narrow like it was made for racing cleats. Inside it held a kit for shining shoes and a few pairs of white cotton gloves. He slipped on an immaculate set that had never been used—first one hand, and then the other.

Then, when he wore these, he turned his attention back to the golden shoe box and fingered the lid. As he lifted it from the front, it hinged in the back and came up like a clamshell to reveal black cloth. Velvet. At first this was all I saw: the black cloth with gold insignias of Jordan Jumpman on it—the familiar silhouette.

Leno turned to me and smiled. "You ready, Jack?"

I found myself bent over, hands above my knees, leaning over him. "I'm sure I am."

"Okay," he said, "feast your eyes on history."

28

The Kicks

Then Leno finally lifted off the top layer of cloth. Underneath I could see the first shoe, the right one. Gold. Here it was with gold around the base of it, bright and shiny, and like it had been laminated with a thin layer of plastic to hold it in place. If Mody had been right about the gold leaf, no one had to worry about it chipping or peeling off.

Leno lifted it carefully out of the box and turned it around slowly.

I knew the original idea for the patent leather had started with a pair of vintage spats, back to Harlem's Cotton Club days, suits and flapper dresses, and I loved the history element of that. On the court, it had never looked anything other than smooth.

Here it shined like gold leaf, the goldest gold, the top of the statehouse in Boston. I could barely believe what I saw. I reached out, and Doc told me, "No."

I could imagine that they might be heavy, hard to wear, but knew Tinker would never have hindered Michael from his game. And yet, they appeared as solid gold to go on your feet. The most beautiful, amazing gold. Like Michael Jackson's "Billy Jean" video, with light-up tiles beneath his every step, only better.

The rest of the distinctive features of the Jordan Eleven were all there: the mesh upper with reinforcements trailing down from the lacing eyelets, all in beige as Mody had said, and sewn into the mesh were jewels of different colors and sizes. Not just sewn in, but some held in by prongs, mounted in individual settings all along the upper, in what could only be called a tasteful way to get this done.

"What is...?"

Leno turned the shoe around and pointed to a spot on the toe where it was scuffed black in a single area. Next to that, MJ had initialed it in a script that I knew.

"Game-worn," he said. "Here's where one of the sheik's goons stepped on Jordan's toe."

Eddie laughed. "Definitely a foul."

I wondered if this was all coming from Mody, if he had created the story of the scuffed toe or merely passed it on from someone else. The signature initials brought me even further into the world of desire, wanting to hold these and have them.

Eddie said, "Only pair like this in existence. Undoubtedly."

Leno smiled. He said, "We did a ton of research on these before backing this venture. Just like we would with any investment. But for these we had to go deep in the crates, so to speak, comb that fricking internet. Dark web. And from what we found, well, there's nothing more definitive than this."

Then he turned the shoe upside down to reveal the bottom, the rubber here gold in color but opaque with a black layer underneath so the familiar silhouette of Jordan walking on air showed through. The bottom had two patches that weren't see-through, and these were gold rubber, with a familiar tread that you could find on any sneaker. Just above the clear rubber along the bottom, where it molded onto the sides, there was a white layer of rubber that led to the gold. Here, on the white, in what looked to be black Sharpie, was a full signature: Michael's.

This, without any question, was Michael Jordan's full name in his own hand.

"Boom," Leno said. "Front on that." A smile had spread across his face, cheek to cheek, and I realized I had one to match it on my own.

I said, "I can't."

There was something friendly in the air of this small back bedroom, as if these brothers and I were now sharing something that went to our childhoods. That was when I understood: we were all still kids inside, wanting to connect to something bigger, something more important than us.

Here we were in the presence of greatness, a singularity, an artifact from the greatest basketball player of all time.

Leno said, "This isn't just hoops history, either. This is the whole sneaker world too. This is *the model* that changed the game entirely from the *shoe* that changed the game. Man, Jordan changed everything. Jordan and Nike. And the Eleven."

Doc said, "Tinker's name on the other one. It's too legit. Too real."

"Legend," Leno said. "Tinker Hatfield, the man who designed the best Nike shoes ever. Air Max, Hurrache, the best Jordans, all of them. Man *invented* cross-trainers. Look him up. Dude was sick with them designs. I *know* you know what I'm talking about. Couldn't grow up when we did and not!"

In the box, the black velvet still covered the other shoe; each was protected in kind. I just shook my head, still wanting to hold them, but now also satisfied to just be in the room, to just see these with my own eyes.

Leno said, "And look at this bejeweling." He pointed to a red stone—a ruby?—set into the mesh toward the toe, then another set along the first lacing. This one was blue—maybe a sapphire? I didn't know enough about stones to have any idea how much these could be worth, but it couldn't have been any small amount. Maybe my cut of their sale, if it ever came to that, would be bigger than I thought.

"Bam!" Leno pointed to the toes, where I saw along the line of stitching a grouping of several diamonds. Not large, but there, clearly announcing their worth.

"You've got to be kidding."

"There it is," Eddie said behind me. "You in the presence of greatness now."

I reached forward. "Can I?"

"Oh, no!" Leno pulled the shoe away. "No, no, no, Jack. That is *not* going to happen."

"Huh uh." Doc grabbed me from behind, held my arms back. "See with your eyes, not with your hands."

"You got oil on your fingers, bro. Stains the leather."

"Okay," I said, "okay."

Leno held the shoe closer so I could see it again. "Check the tongue." He pointed to a black strip of fabric spread across the white tongue. It had writing on it.

He turned the shoe sideways. I had seen the writing on the tongue of the Elevens countless times, never able to make out what it read. What was there had always struck me as an odd series of Greek letters. But now he held it up to me, close to my face, while his brother kept my arms behind my back.

"The key," he said, "is you have to read it sideways. See?" He showed me the tongue, held it even closer now. "On a normal Jordan, it says, 'Jumpman Jordan' here. Now on these, can you read that?"

I worked to make out what I saw. The lettering was very strange, compounded by the fact it stood on its side, kind of flattened. "Looks like 'Saudi Arabia?'"

"Exactly." He pointed to the box, where I presumed the other shoe lay under its cloth protection. "That one says, 'Four Rings.' I assume you know why."

"Ninety-six was the year he won his fourth title."

He showed me the back of the sneaker, where the gold-leaf leather wrapped around. Above that, just to the outside of the seam was a gold brand symbol stitched into the leather, and just beside it, another red stone shining its brightest.

"A ruby?" I asked.

"Rubies," Leno said. "You know it." He pointed out a few other stones along the sides of the shoe.

Then, the last thing he showed me, dead in the middle of the sneaker's back, the familiar number 23 done in small diamonds inlayed into more mesh.

"More diamonds?"

He nodded. "There it is." Then he went to put the shoe back into its box.

"That's it?" I asked. "I don't get to touch it at all?"

"No." He put the sneaker carefully back in the box and tucked the velvet over it and around its sides. He blew a kiss to the sneakers before closing the top of the gold box. Then he pulled out the footlocker, opened that, and put the sneaker box back inside.

"There it is, Jack. Now you seen 'em. Tell us your plan."

Doc let go of my arms. I thought of trying to take them all on right there in the little room, battle my way out, going for the sneakers and the getaway. It was a bad plan, one that would never work.

I sighed. "Okay. Let's talk it all out with Mody first."

29

The Plan

As we passed through the kitchen, I saw them lined up on the couch: Johnny, Momma Koloa, and my man Mody—see no evil, hear no evil, and speak all the evil you could want.

Before I could even get into the living room, Mody started in. "Jack, you seen them now so you know. You know, right?"

"Know what?" I watched Leno and Doc file in behind me. Eddie stood off to the side, staring daggers into the back of my head.

Mody started to get up off the couch, but a look from Johnny kept him in place. "You know what we got to do, now."

"We got to go."

"What?" Now he did stand up, didn't back down even when Johnny and Eddie started toward him. As soon as they laid hands on him, he pushed them away; they tried getting him back down onto the couch but he wasn't having it. "No, fuck this. Hear me out."

They let go. But that was when Leno stepped into the middle of the room and held up his hands. Incredibly, this stopped everything, even Mody's mouth.

Leno said, "Jack Palms here, he's going to make a proposal."

They all waited for me. Even Mody.

"Yeah," I said. "That's my offer. I take Mody back to the mainland, get him back for that bond in San Francisco, and you boys get to keep the shoes. Settle up that debt with the kicks or you guys sell them and pay out what he owes."

"Oh, hells no!" Mody said, and now the brothers physically placed his ass on the couch cushion.

Momma moved over to give him some space. "Watch your mouth now," she told him.

"That's it?" Leno said. "You seen them, now you're willing to let them go?"

"The Jordans?" I showed them my empty hands. "I'm done. My job here is to get this guy back for trial. That's it. That's what I get paid for."

The brothers stood relaxed in front of me, as if an air of tension had left the room. I knew I was looking at a financial hit from letting go of the kicks, and a much younger part of me was dying inside for that, but I wanted the route of far less trouble than messing with the family, Leonardi and Mahogany.

Leno said, "Deal," and he put out his hand to shake.

Mody stood up again. "The fuck is this? I get cut out like an asshole? Do you all recognize what I did to get those? Those are my grails, man."

I shook Leno's hand. "You'll give him a cut, right? If the sale goes over what he owes."

They laughed. But their mother stepped forward. "I'll see that they do," she said.

"Where you gonna sell them?" Mody asked. "You'll get stripped on the web with these. No way they can go on eBay. Do you even know *how* to sell something like these? They *have to* go to the right buyer. This is history."

Leno shrugged. "Maybe I just keep them. Consider the debt squashed."

"Oh, Jesus." Mody held a hand toward Momma Koloa before she could respond. "Sorry. But no way. These are too big a thing. There's one place they have to be sold. You got to take them to New York. To SneakerCon."

Now the brothers laughed harder. "Fuck that," Johnny said, then got kicked in the calf by his mother. He said, "Sorry, bro. But I don't leave Kauai."

"Jack can sell it." Mody smiled in a way that made my skin crawl. His eyes were crazier than I'd seen them. Lack of sleep had to be catching up with him.

"Not me," I said. "I'm staying put in SF when I get back home."

"I'll work on him." Mody winked at the brothers. "Jack would be the perfect guy to do it. And imagine the payday we could get. I'm talking about…" Here he paused, as if he were trying to imagine the number it'd take to get us all interested, or counting the jewels in his head, or figuring digits on a mental abacus. Then he came out with, "A million. A million dollars."

I was about to say I'd go to New York for that kind of money, even a cut of it, but the brothers didn't like the idea, even at that price.

"No way," Leno said. "We've heard enough from your mouth. From now on, we take care of this on our own."

I could see from the way Leno looked at me and how he treasured the sneakers that they weren't going to put them in my hands. Shit, they wouldn't even let me touch the box. And I wasn't sure I blamed them, either. Something about those Jordans—*the Maltese*—made me think I'd keep them for myself if I were in the same position.

And still, the million dollars had started my own mental abacus rolling, beads popping left to right all over the frame. I was curious as all get out, planned to Google and find out as much about the market for rare sneakers as I could, as soon as I had the chance.

I cuffed the back of Mody's neck with my hand, aiming him toward the door. "Airport, brother. Now. You heard the man."

"Mother fuck!" He squared off against me, ready to go down swinging or die trying.

Momma Koloa reached to swat him across the back of his head. She barely made his shoulder. "Enough talk like that. You listen to the reason now, boy! Listen to my Leno and what he's saying to you."

"Oh, no. No way." Mody started shaking his head, vibrating all over like he might burst. "All this for nothing? No freaking way. I must have those. They're mine!"

This was where I earned my keep, I figured, made good on my role as enforcer for Joe Leonardi and the courts back in SF. I stepped in with a right jab and snapped Mody's head back fast, then hit him in the solar plexus with an open-palm right. He wheezed—I was starting to like this strike, and its effects—and then Eddie took hold of him from behind.

I showed him what the right hook would look like—where it would come from and what part of my fist his face would meet—and that was enough. He raised his hands, as much as he could with Eddie holding him. You knock the wind out of a guy like that, it can take away his whole fight.

"Whatever, man. Just whatever." He looked like he might really lose it, like he might be the most beaten man in the world.

But the Koloas seemed okay with it, ready to take that at face value. They even filed over one at a time to hug Mody goodbye. There was no animosity among them in the end, even if they'd pushed Mody to commit a crime and get on the wrong side of the wrong people in San Francisco. Here on the island, it was all about love. Not that Mody was happy with the turn of events.

They pushed him out of the house, and I led him toward the Jeep. He swore himself silly, talking about all the work he'd done to get the sneakers, finding them, sending countless emails to the Saudi seller to line up the trade, all of it, all the way to the car.

"And now all this for nothing?" he said.

"Come on, man." I pushed him up into the passenger seat and buckled the belt around him. If nothing else it would slow him enough for me to make a grab, hit him, do enough damage to stop an escape. I said, "Sometimes you just got to play the hand that you're dealt. Fold even. It's got to be about the long game, man. Don't you see that by now? Take care of your shit and live to fight another day." I stood by his side of the Jeep, watched to see how that went over.

"What?" He looked at me like I was crazy. "You believe that shit?"

"Something like that. Maybe. Doesn't matter, because I'm not the one with the L.A. family mad at me and an outstanding bond one ocean away."

He didn't say anything else.

"You hear that?" I asked him.

"Hear what?"

I held my hand to my ear. "That silence? That's your future calling. Any fucking thing could happen. You want to be around to see what comes?"

He turned around in his seat to face forward. Maybe he was finally listening to reason. Maybe he was cooking up another insane plan. I didn't care. I walked around the hood to get us on the road to Lihue Airport. Then we'd be gone.

30

Rabbit Hole

Getting Mody to the airport was the easy part. He slumped in his seat the whole way, even through the return of the rental Jeep. When I asked him how he planned to get his own Jeep returned, he said he didn't really care.

"Maybe Mack will do me that solid," he said.

"One can hope."

Waiting in line for the agriculture check, he moped about leaving the Jordans behind, and barely talked during security and boarding.

In the gate area, I texted Leonardi that we were on our way. He wrote back to say he'd call off the dogs. I knew that applied to Mahogany. I hoped it meant the family, as well; we didn't need anyone looking for Mody at the other end of our flight, trying to take payment out of his ass for what he'd done. I knew Leonardi wouldn't want that, either. Self-interest: that was his MO. Having Mody make it back to court was all he wanted.

On the flight, I put Mody in the window seat and took the aisle. We were lucky enough that the middle seat stayed open. As far as I knew, Mody hadn't slept the night before. Now he pulled the navy blue airplane blankets around him, stuck a few pillows under his head, and dozed off.

I took the opportunity to open up my computer, pay for the in-flight wifi and see what I could find online about sneaker collecting, Air Jordans, and where someone might pick up something like the shoes we'd just left behind, even if they were irreplaceable and completely priceless.

I also wanted to see if I could find any mention of their existence.

I started with eBay and found hundreds of Jordans, even thousands, that looked like the ones I'd known way back when. These Retros, done in all colorways, came out all the time, even weekly—I found that out by looking at the Jumpman 23 Twitter handle from the Jordan brand. The colors I knew from childhood were called OG Colorways, and that was just the tip of what you could find now. I couldn't believe all the different, newly made Jordans that I saw. And what's more? I wanted to start buying some in my size right away.

The authentic relics of Nike and Jordan's heyday, what Mody seemed especially into, had a set of sites all their own. Websites with names like Sneaker Freaker, Kicks Addict, Sneakerhead.com and, strangely, Flight Club. These were the true halls of the elite sneaker addict like Mody. A lot of the sites featured Jordans prominently. When I saw the prices, I started getting some idea of the world I was working my way into. Some of the Jordans *started* as low as $400 for adult sizes, and they went up from there. Even versions for babies or toddlers cost more than $200. Even for reissues. Crazy.

For the original sneakers, prices ran higher. Much higher. I wasn't surprised that some sellers still had 1990s-era sneakers in pristine condition, tissue-paper-wrapped in their boxes, but the idea that some were worth $30k kind of blew me away.

"Fuck."

A man and woman feeding strawberries to their child gave me a harsh look from across the aisle. I waved them off. No other logical way to react to a price like that for a shoe. Some of these were basically museum pieces.

I kept looking, trying to find anything about a pair connected to Saudi Arabia, Malta or anything like that. If there were such a thing, it was so rarified that I couldn't find information on it using a few basic internet searches. I had no inkling of where I might find those videos of the king's game that Leno Koloa had shown me, either. They basically did not exist.

A half-hour later, I pushed back from the laptop and forced myself to look away. I'd gone so far down a website rabbit hole that I was close to finding the shoe version of a Mad Hatter. It was crazy that such a wide world of collectors, sellers and old sneakers existed.

I'd found videos of NBA players showing off their closets of sneakers, countless Jordans arranged neatly on rows that they bragged about, delighting in how rare some of their pairs were. The fewer copies of a given shoe that were made, the more original, the higher its value and the more of a prize it became.

There was some guy online called the Mayor who had a whole room in his house full of rare sneakers kept in clear plastic containers—no boxes. He said he had several hundred thousand dollars' worth of kicks, from Jordans, to other Nikes, to brands I'd never heard of with all-red bottoms. And this guy just looked like some schmuck in a bucket hat, a nobody.

He made a point in one video of bending a sneaker, creasing

the toe-box of a rare Jordan Four designed by Eminem and Carhartt. The real Eminem, not the one sleeping next to me. Supposedly these kicks were worth $25k.

Even the richest people, the most famous—even NBA players—still had sneakers they couldn't get their hands on, ones they were looking to find.

In one case, a particular pair of game-worn Michael Jordan twelves from his "flu game"—this was in the 1997 finals against Utah, when he scored 38 points with a fever and basically had to be carried off the court at time outs by Scottie Pippen—these kicks, *signed*, had wound up in the hands of a Jazz ball boy who held them for sixteen years and then sold them for over $105,000. Amazing. I'd heard all of Mody's talk, and this was the first inkling of what the Maltese Jordans might really command.

It blew my mind. I mean, I'd heard Mody's claim of a million, but who had any idea whether what came out of his mouth was ever true?

I found that the sneaker world was one that didn't expose itself easily to newcomers or outsiders. Comment threads on some sites were password-protected or carried out in lingo so obscure that I couldn't tell what anyone was saying. Some entry barrier of coolness had been electronically constructed here, and I couldn't find my way through it.

"No Non-Addicts Allowed," one of the sites boasted across its homepage, which was empty unless you could log in.

When I let my eyes adjust, I saw Mody was wide-awake and grinning at me.

"I see you're descending into my world. Be careful. It'll ruin your life."

"Trying to. It's not so welcoming to outsiders."

"A reason for that. Here, let me see." He held his hands open for my laptop, and I passed it, let him open his tray table and set it up to use. He accessed a few sites I hadn't seen, popped into back-door entries, and started showing me around what I hadn't been able to gain access to.

"Even for the guys with money," he started, "we're not looking to just sell these things to *anyone*. It's got to be word of mouth at least. Check this out."

He turned the screen toward me, showing me a page with the backstory of the Maltese Jordans, here called the "Saudi Arabian Elevens" complete with a few grainy pictures of Jordan on a basketball court somewhere, presumably signing the exact pair I had seen that morning. They were them, so far as I could tell, and it was definitely *him*. Men in traditional Saudi dress flanked him on both sides, as well as a short guy with a baseball hat I recognized as Tinker Hatfield.

"What site is this?"

"Sneaker Addict. I started looking around for any info about the Elevens when I first got word of them a few years ago. This was the only site that had pictures. I don't even know if these were supposed to be taken, but like the shoes themselves, they were probably meant for the king's private collection and then got out later."

"How the...?" I wanted to ask questions but didn't know where to begin. What did I want to know most? What was I supposed to believe and understand implicitly?

"You're getting into it," Mody said. "I can tell. You're one of us."

"I'm not like you," I said. "No chance. But I know the legends I grew up watching, and Jordan was one of them. And I love this pair of sneakers—the Elevens, I mean. I remember Iverson wearing them at Georgetown when he was a little outlaw, dunking on everybody, even as the smallest guy on the court."

Mody smiled. "Fucking lovely. So you know."

"Anyone our age, how could they not? But to this level?" I pointed at the screen. "And back there? That's fucking crazy. You're far gone."

Mody sat back in his chair. He folded his arms across his chest. "Maybe."

"Listen," I said. "You know who backs the firm you stole from in San Francisco? The fucking mob. You do not want to get into them for anything. *Especially* if the alternative is the Koloas. Those guys? Come on."

"I had to do it, Jack. I don't expect you to understand." What he said next was as simple and true as anything could be. I understood exactly what he meant. "The Koloas had my J's." He turned to me with a fresh honesty in his eye. "To come this close? No way. I need those, Jack. And we left them."

For a second I thought he was going to cry, but of course that was crazier than anything. Grown men don't cry. Especially not about sneakers, no matter what.

He sat quietly for a bit. Then he said, "Think of it like a Holy Grail. What would be the one thing you'd leave everything in your life for? What's the one thing you'd give everything to get?"

I looked down the length of the plane, rows of heads nodding off, watching movies on the hang-down screens, reading or viewing other movies on laptops and various devices. I wanted to say something about my career in Los Angeles, how it felt to be on those screens and to be the person that everyone recognized, looked up to, wanted to impress. I thought I should say something about how it was to feel welcomed in the world like that, but the truth was it was more strange than anything, more awkward and impersonal than good. I missed the work of it: being on set and catered to, having everyone wait for me to say my lines and act, perform. I missed performing more than anything, really, that escape into the not-knowing and creating the character from what I felt was right. I missed creating.

But would I give everything to get it back?

No.

I had given everything just from having it. Gotten too close to having it all, and then slipped down the backside of that slope. Lost too much. Now? Now I knew there was only so much in a given day—the work, the light, the air and the feelings—to know that I was lucky just to have what I did. And did I want any *thing*? No, my Fastback was the thing I coveted most. It had changed and grown with me, come through scathed, shot, repainted and altered. I had given it so much. But still: was it something that gave me all that value?

No, it was just that: a thing.

I understood where Mody was coming from with his desire to hold that piece of history, a beautiful item with a direct connection to a man who'd risen to the level of a God, but I knew too that Jordan was just a man. The gambling, the baseball, and who knows what else? He was just one damned-competitive son of a bitch who on certain days could fly; a man who played a game better than anyone else had ever. He was a hero.

But still.

Was there one thing I'd give everything to get?

No. Of that I was sure. Right then and there, I could not imagine what that one thing would be. Not even the Fastback. Not anymore, assuming I didn't have it, or if I somehow had to get it back. At this point in my life, maybe even the Fastback I could let go.

Maybe.

I looked back to Mody. "No," I lied. "I guess there isn't."

31

The Dream

Mody said "I guess that's what separates us, then. I have this dream. The thing I want more than anything else is those shoes."

"To sell them?"

"Maybe." He shrugged.

And I knew then he was going to lie; that to the true collector it's just the having, the owning that makes everything complete. He would do what he could and lose what he had to be somewhere, perhaps on that island, possessing the singular pair of shoes. Just holding them.

It made no sense. But then, there it was.

"Yeah, I'd sell them. Got to do it to get you your cut, right Jack?"

"Definitely." I took the laptop back off his tray table and set it on mine, closed the top. Maybe I'd go back over these websites later, extending my curiosity. But I got where Mody was coming from, and now I knew the real danger.

I wasn't surprised at what he said next.

He said, "So you know I've got to get to New York, then. I'm just telling you now to make it plain. Either you're with me, or I go my own way. There's not a way you can stop me."

I thought about the airport, how he could make a scene and my best bet would be to subdue him, how that could go wrong more ways than it could go right. I wasn't a professional, didn't have a license, and truth be told, what was I really going to do about getting Mody to Leonardi if he happened to make a complete and unruly fuss? It would lead to trouble for us both.

The airport was not going to be a good place for us.

I didn't give in, but I asked what I thought was the most important question. "How do you know they'll bring the sneakers there?"

"Just that they will. I know them. Of course. There's not any other option. Now that they know the convention is happening, they'll go there to sell the shoes."

"And?"

"And that's when I'll get them back. Unfamiliar environment, strange setting, lots of buying and selling and strange characters around. That's the time to make my move."

"But if they…?"

"They'll sell them. Trust me. They just want the money. It's too much for them not to."

"And you don't?"

"I want the shoes. Just the shoes."

I said, "It's gotta be the shoes, money."

"Shoes and money, shoes or money. Call me Mars Blackmon, okay? It's all good."

"There's a bail out for you in San Francisco. I mention that to the police, they cuff you, we go right to the Hall of Justice. And Leonardi likes that."

He pursed his lips, thinking it through. What did I know?

Bluff or real, I didn't know if I could get him out of the airport on my own, or if I wanted the mess of finding out.

"Say I had a friend meeting us at the airport, Jack, someone willing to hand you enough money to make it worth your while, the kind of dough to let you look the other way on this. What would you say then?"

"No thanks. Or fuck that. Take your pick."

"Right." He thought it over again. "Well said. I get you."

He folded a blanket then and tucked it in between his head and the plane's wall, closed his eyes. Soon he was breathing deeply, either as a ploy or for real. I kept both eyes open. Sure, I needed sleep too, but that could wait. This was the job.

I emailed Leonardi from my computer that we were approaching SFO, when we'd get in and our flight info. I said to be waiting or to send someone to get us, because Mody was going to try and run, again.

I'll do my best, I wrote, *but I don't want to find out what a desperate man will resort to.*

We were about two hours outside of SFO when I finally dozed. It wasn't a big nap, just a head-on-the-hand blink, really, which was all I had space for in my seat. I woke up when Mody tried to step over me into the aisle, then pushed him back down into his seat.

"You wait," I said. "Once we're there you can go."

Maybe there wasn't much he could do on a plane in the middle of the sky over open water, but I didn't want to find out. I pictured myself working with a stewardess to get him out of a locked bathroom, and that was more than I wanted.

"Just sit."

He sat again, re-tucked the blanket under his ear and closed his eyes. He was plotting something, I knew, but what?

I pictured Leonardi steaming mad in his office, calling Mahogany on the phone or setting up something even more nefarious. If the family knew we were coming in, and they wanted to make a play, it would take much more than Mahogany to get us out of the airport alive.

I waved down the stewardess on her next pass, asked her to bring me a double order of coffee, black.

32

Landing

When the plane landed, Mody stared out the window rather than make eye contact or communicate with me. He finally asked me if he could check his phone, and I acquiesced, though I didn't want him contacting anyone. I watched him real close.

As soon as he turned off the airplane mode, I saw he had one text message that came in.

"What is it?" I asked.

He read the phone and then clicked away from what he'd read.

"What's what?"

"That message?"

He fast-scrolled to the top of his messages with whomever had just written and deleted the whole conversation, just cleared it right out.

"What message?"

"Right," I said. "Nice."

Maybe I shouldn't have let him check his phone. But what did I know?

"Give me that," I told him, and when he handed over the phone, I dialed in my own number—always good to have a suspect's phone number if you needed it—let it ring through, and then turned it completely off. They could track people using cell phone signals these days, and if Leonardi didn't have Mody's cell to begin with, that didn't mean someone else didn't. If the mob was connected to his former employers, they'd know it for sure.

That, and maybe mine, too.

I saved Mody's number in my contacts, checked my messages—text, phone and any last emails—and then wrote a fast text to Leonardi telling him our flight from Lihue had landed. Then I turned off my phone. Who knew what the damned trackers were capable of now? Not this guy.

We reached the gate, the seatbelt sign dinged off, and the passengers started scrambling for the overheads to get their luggage. I watched Mody in his chair, not moving, and he followed my lead.

"Whatever you say, Jack," he told me.

"Just be clear with me. What're you planning?"

He laughed, short and grunty. "Not a chance. *If* I'm planning something."

"For your sake, I almost hope you are. Because if the mob is out there waiting, they're going to be a lot worse on you than I've been."

"A big if, Jack."

"Either way, you're not getting away from me here." I put a death grip on his forearm, crushed it tight. "We get off this thing once everyone else has, hear me?"

He nodded.

We waited. Most of the others on the flight were your run-of-the-mill tourists: families, couples, people excited to get away at first and now sad to be home. They had a monotone vibe to them but for the fact that some of them seemed to be San Franciscans and some were heading for a connecting flight to get them home.

I turned my phone back on. Better to hear from Joe Leonardi if he were close than to worry about someone tracking me. I was about to be in the airport. Probably something that anyone interested knew.

Then our rows and the rows around us had cleared and the stewardesses started to look at us funny. I pulled Mody up onto his feet.

"Go time."

I pushed him ahead of me up the aisle toward the front door of the plane, expecting him to make a move. With the other passengers in front of us, however, he had nowhere to go.

I grabbed my backpack out of the overhead and followed him toward the door. As we walked to the front, I watched the stewardess and the pilot wishing everyone a good day, safe travels. That was, until they saw Mody. I couldn't see what he was about to do, but something in their faces conveyed a fear I didn't miss.

As soon as he reached the stewardess, he grabbed her and pushed her toward me. I called his name, not wanting him to actually make this play, but he was.

He sure fucking was.

33

Runner

Outside in the walkway, Mody cut out the side door by pushing one of the ground crew into a wall. The guy had just been unloading someone's baby stroller and now he was on his ass, with Mody through the door.

I followed.

The stewardess wasn't hard to get past; she dove away from me, and the pilots pulled her to safety. "Get that asshole," one of them said.

In the tunnel, I went for the door and saw Mody's mistake right away: he was taking the stairs like a runner instead of like a street kid on the move.

What can I say? I learned a thing or two about how to run from subway police growing up in Boston. I vaulted onto the portable staircase's railing, mounted it sidesaddle and slid down after Mody.

I caught him at the bottom—my legs hit him mid-back and sent him flying face-first onto the tarmac. A cart with trailers of luggage swerved to avoid running him over, spilling a few suitcases as it did.

"Fucking Jack," he stammered, righting himself onto his

hands and getting up. "This is bigger than me, bigger than either of us. Let me go."

He turned to run, and I full-on tackled him, jumped on his back and wrapped him up, sending us both onto a moving trailer of luggage.

"Just give up," I said. "This won't work."

I pried one of his hands off a suitcase and twisted his arm behind his back. Face down, he cried for me to stop, but I held him tight. The cart-driver realized we were there and that he'd dumped a few bags of his precious cargo, so he stopped short, basically popping us off. I pulled Mody onto his feet.

"The fuck was that?" I asked him. "Really?"

He stared at his feet, either from the shame of his brief attempt or a refusal to discuss it, I wasn't sure.

"You can't be out here," the cart driver said to us as he walked around the wagons to pick up bags and restore them to their rightful conveyance. He bent and lifted one, two of them and tossed each onto a pile carelessly. "Best get back on up them stairs." He pointed back toward the plane from which we'd come.

When I looked back up, I checked the walkway to our gate and saw the row of windows on the concourse filled with faces pressed up against the glass. Apparently we'd made quite a show. Then, among the viewers, I saw what I didn't want to see: four guys with thick necks wearing dark suits, white-collared shirts unbuttoned, standing at the windows eyeing us with intent. Two had their hands on the glass like they wanted to pound it out and jump down to the tarmac. These were not friends of Leonardi; that was clear. But somehow our arrival information had slipped out or gotten passed along to somebody—a person, or persons, who wanted Mody's ass.

Much as I knew about Leonardi and what he'd want, what I thought he'd want, sometimes the San Francisco Family had a way of accomplishing things on its own. So there they were, and I did not like their welcome party. I wasn't going to let them chisel me out of my bounty, either.

A thought occurred to me: that we could avoid our destination gate and maybe even the whole terminal. Making a fast break for another part of the airport could keep us away from our new friends and eager escorts.

"Gentlemen, you have to come back up here!" It was the stewardess, standing outside of our ramp with a baggage handler and a security agent. They all three watched us to see what we'd do.

"Get ready," I told Mody, releasing his arm.

I could hear the surprise in his voice when he said, "Ready for what?"

"*To run.*" I pulled him to me and told him if he didn't follow, I'd feed him to the mob boys myself. Then I let him go and jumped into a sprint across the wide expanse of planes, luggage carts and trucks. The handler behind us yelled something, and I imagined the suits inside scattering for the chase.

Mody must have finally come around and sensed the danger; he chose to follow my line around the first luggage cart and toward the adjacent terminal. A moving plane headed toward us, an Alaskan Airlines number with a big Inuit face painted along its flank. For the first time in my life I was on foot outside a moving, full-sized airliner, judging the height of its wheelbase and whether I'd be able to run underneath. This was a new and interesting proposition, to say the least. Definitely something that fit better in a movie. And here it was, my life!

The bigger issue was whether the plane would move at the right speed for us to pass between the fore and aft wheels as we ran. Sometimes there's no time for a choice of right or left, fast or slow; it just amounts to *yes*—plow ahead and move forward into the world—or no, curl up and suck your thumb. I chose *yes*, hoping Mody would keep up.

I slowed for a moment to let the front wheels pass, then dashed far enough under the plane to be sure the right rear wheels would miss me. If I never felt like a bug before, here was my first quintessential Kafkaesque experience. Ducking even lower under the body for good measure, I kept on, running until I could see it made more sense to slow and let the left rear wheels pass me by. I did and came out the far side with a luggage cart heading straight for me. I checked fast, saw Mody about five steps behind, and darted behind the cart, then around a fuel truck and beneath a plane parked at a gate. Somewhere along the length of the terminal wall, I hoped to find an unlocked door.

I hit the first door I saw and yanked at the handle: *locked*. Ran down to my left, tried another: same thing. Now I could see two of the suits at the runway, looking both ways to gauge the paths of planes. Too slow, too cautious.

Mody caught up to me, out of breath but yelling, "Who the fuck are those thugs?"

"*La Familia*," I called over my shoulder. "Remember when I warned you about them?"

I made the next door and found it unlocked, opened it, went

in, and held it behind me for Mody to follow.

He came along, unaware how close the suits were to seeing where we'd gone. I slammed the door behind us and turned to find some sort of industrial off-limits level of baggage handling, conveyor belts, and carts cruising through. A driver passed us by with a slight wave, responding as though he could care less that we were here.

"Where we headed?" Mody asked.

"I don't know."

"New York," he said. "That's where we need to be."

I wanted to smack him again, but didn't. "Give me some sense of how we make that happen."

He looked at me blankly, shrugged. "I thought you were in charge."

"In charge of getting you back to jail. That's what we make happen. You have a date with Joe Leonardi, remember?"

I grabbed his shoulder and pushed Mody in front of me, taking him away from the door we'd come in through, continuing on our line. He kept talking, spouting ideas about getting on another flight, heading right to New York City, and tracking down the Koloas to see what they'd do next with the shoes.

"You got to be kidding," I said, finally. I stopped where I was and pointed back toward the runway. "Did you not see the guys out there coming after us? Do you not realize these are *not* the guys you want to fuck with? At this point, your safest place is in prison. Hear me?"

His head fell. Dejected, he tried one last request, "But you'll go for me, won't you?"

I answered with a smack across his face. "Shut up and keep moving."

34

Mahogany

We made it through the underbelly of Terminal 3, then found our way out past baggage claim and grabbed the first cab we saw. Luckily all the cabs took credit cards now. Given what I'd added to Gina's stash from my own pockets, I was long-since out of money.

And credit was easier to bill back to Joe Leonardi later.

We rode straight to his office on Bryant, right across from the Hall of Justice. I don't think Mody had any idea where he was about to wind up.

When we walked into Leonardi's office, he stood up at his desk and walked around it to greet us. He was pumping my hand almost before I got in the door.

"Fucking Jack. I knew I could count on you to get this bastard." He caught Mody by the back of his neck and pushed him farther into the office, either toward the holding cell I knew he had in the back, or at a chair for him to sit down.

"That's why you threatened me with Mahogany?"

"Nah, nah." He waved it off, or tried to. For me, his threat hung in the air like a bad fart, one that would stick to him for a while. "Just jokes, Jack. Jokes."

A door opened in the second half of the office, one of the private rooms for discussing the finer details of bond payments. Out walked Mahogany, wearing a thin white blouse tucked into a slim skirt that fell below her knees, the kind that would keep any woman from so much as hurrying. Her straight brown hair fell to her shoulders. Her lips pushed forward in their permanent pout. Underneath that blouse I could see enough of her black camisole to make me want more, enough so you wanted to stare and either did, or had to look away to protect your dignity. Such was her power over us.

"Oh, I know that retainer we spoke of wasn't a joke, Joey." She winked at me as Leonardi crumpled. I didn't know anyone else who could get away with calling him 'Joey.' "You are paying me right now, *aren't you?*"

Leonardi laughed. He didn't have much choice. "Kidding," he said. "All around. Ms. Mahogany and I were just having a friendly meeting here to discuss business. Business which is very good for us all now that Mr. Mody has returned to secure his bail." He tapped his watch.

Mody huffed. He fell into an office chair and tilted back. "I'm never going to get the shoes, am I?"

"No, like I've been telling you."

"What's this about shoes?" Leonardi asked. "Is this about all those pairs we found up at your place in Tiburon?"

Mody blanched. "Those? Fuck it. Keep 'em."

I said, "He's talking about his own white whale. The Holy Grail of kicks."

"Whatever. Unless he plans on trying out for the San Quentin hoops team, he won't be needing any Jordans where he's heading."

Leonardi walked over to stand behind Mody. He forced his chair back to its original position, pushing Mody's feet onto the ground. Then he said, "Let me help you here," and slapped a handcuff over Mody's wrist. He tightened the other cuff around the chair's arm.

"Join us," Leonardi said. "We hope you'll stay a while."

Mahogany turned her heavily mascaraed gaze on me. "White whale?"

"He's a sneakerhead." I nodded at Mody. She took it all in, raising her eyebrows at Mody's feet. I added, "Despite the flip-flops."

"Sneakerhead with a Holy Grail? Some kind of a Jordan thing?"

"Exactly. He calls them the Maltese Jordans."

She laughed. "No," she said. "Really. *Really?*"

I gave her my serious face with a slight smile, like how could anyone make up something like that, and she nodded as if that explained it all. From there I kept my mouth shut. The fewer people who knew the legend of the Maltese Jordans, the better. At least before they made their big splash in New York.

Mahogany clapped Leonardi on the back. "Well my man, looks like you two have this all under control." She headed toward the door, high heels sounding sharply on the floor. "I'll send you a bill."

I smiled at her as she walked past. As easy as she was on the eyes, I couldn't resist.

"Adios, trooper," she told me.

I held the door open as she left, then let it close gently behind her. Joe Leonardi's jaw was hanging on his chest.

"What is it about that woman?" he asked.

"How about let's talk about *my* bill, Joey."

35

Hypebeast

I got back to my apartment later than I wanted. After a few days on the island, even working, it didn't feel great to be home. The air in my living room was stale, the mail piled up behind the door was all bills, and the fog had rolled in early, making my bare legs cold.

The city was still the city.

I was exhausted from all the excitement, the all-nighter, and the flight, so I was practically asleep by the time I flopped myself onto the bed. I did the mental math and figured I'd slept less than eight hours in the past two days combined.

I dreamed in fitful sleep, broken by nightmares of mafia hitmen banging on my door, island fat boys breaking down my bed, and more sneakers than any man could ever want to imagine.

In the morning, I made strong coffee and pulled my laptop up onto the glass kitchen table. Before I knew it, I was doing a search for the sneaker convention in New York City. Whatever pulled me to it, I didn't know. Maybe I just let my fingers do the walking. Either way, there I was, looking at the lineup for that Saturday afternoon at the Marriott Marquis.

And honestly, I wanted a few pairs of those new-release, retro Air Jordans of my own.

The SneakerCon website promised over 10,000 sneakerheads in attendance and "hundreds of thousands of sneakers." Its Twitter feed linked to articles about the "flu game" Jordans, a few of the super-rare releases that involved collaborations between either celebrities or famous boutique designers, something called "Yeezy Red Octobers," and a handful of other things I couldn't make sense of.

But the sums, the monetary figures I saw for pairs of unworn sneakers had me considering that Mody might have been right in the end about what the Maltese Jordans could fetch at the Con. Hardly anything else mentioned Jordan's playing days, nothing that involved the man himself actually putting his feet inside the shoes. These sneakers, Mody's, if they were really the stuff of legend, myth, mystery and history, and if the pictures I'd seen could back up their story, then maybe these were as big as Mody had said. Or bigger.

I wondered who else knew about those videos I'd seen and the pictures, and how many of those people would be in New York.

Or maybe I just needed to drink my coffee, get to the gym and go back to my old life. Leonardi had padded my bank account, picked up my expenses, and as long as the mafia didn't come calling, I was in far better shape than I had been when I'd gotten his call a few days before.

Time to just go back to my old life, right?

But something had a hook in me, way down deep where I didn't have a chance of prying it free.

It was 5:30 by the time I pried myself away from the computer. I'd been on eBay, Sneaker Addict, Hypebeast, and sites documenting the upcoming SneakerCon as well as a few past ones in Oakland, LA, and New Orleans.

I'd seen Air Jordans on eBay, even placed a few guilty bids on a pair of Bred Elevens released a year before and some "Oreo" Fives. I could already see myself going downhill, picking out other models I wanted, trying to recreate my ideal collection from high school and college. There would definitely be some money spent in my near future—online and also at my local Union Square Niketown.

I'd read whatever I could find on a host of sports sites documenting details of Jordan's career and its highlights. I'd watched YouTube videos of him torching Kobe, battling Bird, and talking so much trash you'd need a dumpster to haul it. To say I'd gone down a rabbit hole was an understatement. I couldn't believe how fast the time had passed.

What I'd found didn't surprise me: beyond the crazy prices for new Jordan releases online, original releases from the '90s sold for thousands if they were in good condition. Anything signed by Jordan raised the price again by thousands. Game-worn was a whole other category altogether. Soon the pair he'd worn in a 1996 finals game—when he *didn't* have the flu—started seeming like a bargain at just $27k. But what intrigued me most was finding independent references, both oblique and direct, to a trip Jordan had taken to the Middle East in the summer of '96. There wasn't much mention of what he'd done there, but one or two old blog posts hinted at Jordan's need to pick up some big cash to pay off a gambling debt without letting his then-wife or the Chicago Bulls find out.

So it didn't seem implausible that he may have actually played in a game for the Saudi king's entertainment. And that was just before he made the movie *Space Jam* with Warner Brothers. If you agreed to do a movie with Bugs, Taz, Daffy, and Foghorn Leghorn, you definitely needed money. Having been in the movie business myself, I could appreciate the mercenary status of doing a project like *Space Jam*.

I stood up and walked around the kitchen. The coffee maker held its spot on the narrow counter between the stove and the fridge, right by my fourth-floor window. Outside, cars honked on the avenues below. In the living room, I did pushups on the hardwood floor between the coffee table and the TV. Three sets of twenty-five. It felt good to get some blood flowing. I tried a few of the exercises Chan had taught me: stretches and a few poses he'd taken from tai chi.

After dressing for a run—track pants and Nikes that now looked way too boring to be seen in—I headed outside and down to the Embarcadero to get in a couple of miles. I almost left my phone, didn't want to hear anything from Joe Leonardi or anyone out of North Beach, but finally I took it for the music.

As I ran, I had a hard time not thinking about the Jordans, the Koloas, Gina, even Mody. I wondered if I would see her again, and whether Mody would spend a few years behind bars. Sure, he was safer on the inside, but maybe he wasn't—the family undoubtedly had the power to reach him.

If I cared about Mody as a friend, which I didn't, I could try to save him. But that was a non-starter. Where would I even begin? What would it look like? I didn't know.

Even if he got some of the money from the Maltese, you don't buy off the San Francisco family or pay down their anger. No, you fuck with them, you get the stick. And Mody had certainly fucked with them when he embezzled from a firm they backed.

So what did I care? His problem, not mine.

But my problems were the old ones I'd always had: something inside of me wanting more. More what? A bigger bank account, maybe another car? Sure, even trying to strip it all down to the simple life, that had led me to find my own limitations. No matter how many ways I tried to rationalize it, my thoughts kept taking me back to one thing: the Jordans and a chance of getting them in New York City. Being in on that deal.

I couldn't give it up.

Part III

The Con

Money, it's gotta be the shoes.

36

Let's Go

On the back end of my run, I stopped in at Niketown, the same one that used to have my boy Tom Brady draped all the way up its side. Up on the fifth floor, I found their Air Jordans section. They had nothing of interest in my size, and when I asked about the recent releases I'd seen online, they told me those ones sold out within an hour, sometimes even less. What they did have, on display behind glass, was a collection of every Air Jordan model made during MJ's NBA career, all on display in a row. Every sneaker, every year, with the model number, date, and career highlights. Every one of them was all white. Not a touch of color on a one. Why? I have no idea. I'd never seen these for sale and didn't want them, but seeing them all lined up like that, representing all the pairs, it made my heart flutter.

By the time I got home, I had decided to call Gina.

She picked up less than a minute after the bartender at the Sheraton went to find her, started in with, "This better not be Jack Palms."

"You know it is," I said. "And aren't you even a little bit glad to hear from me?"

I could hear the crickets chirping across the wide ocean, the empty sound of dead air in my own apartment.

"That bad?"

"I thought it would at least take you a few days to get tired of missing me and call. Are you that desperate? Am I that ingrained in your mind?"

I knew better than to say it was the sneakers, not her. Somewhere along the line, I'd learned at least that much. But I didn't waste her time or mine; I cut right to it, the angle I thought she'd be into. "What if I propose a way you can make some money? Call it the other part of what you never got from that North Shore bar. Maybe we triple that."

"I'm listening."

"Those guys I went to see. The Koloas. You know anything about where they might be now? Think you can look into that?"

She clicked her tongue. "I can look into it. Depending. We talking at least a few G's here?"

"If you can give me a status on all four of them for the rest of the week, I'll pay you more than a few G's."

"Let me talk to a few people. I'll call you back."

She hung up before I could tell her how to reach me, but that was how things worked these days. And Gina? Gina had always had my number.

She called me two days later. "The young one," she said. "He's flying to New York City."

"What?" She'd caught me in the middle of watching a replay of the prior night's Warriors game. Steph Curry was lighting it up, even if Mark Jackson kept putting him in sets where he couldn't operate on his own.

"You heard me," she said. "The little Koloa. Leno. He booked a flight."

I was up off the couch before she could finish, headed back toward my bedroom closet and the small suitcase I kept there.

She asked, "You still there?"

"I am." I unzipped it and tossed in a few T-shirts. "And also I'm *there*."

"I'm coming," she said.

"What?" I stopped what I was doing, held up with two pairs of boxers in my hand.

"I need the adventure," she said, "and I want in."

"In on what?"

"Don't even think about thinking about bullshitting me, Jack. I know something big is going down, and I want my piece. You'll need an extra pair of hands. And tits." She laughed. "Tell me I couldn't smooth over some buyers in New York."

"What buyers?" I sat down on the bed. Her extra pair of hands might come in useful. Her tits, on the other hand... I wanted them all to myself.

"This is about those Jordans, Jack. Don't shit me. SneakerCon is coming up this weekend, and that's the place to take Mody's dream pair."

I wondered how she had put it all together and what else she knew. But I didn't ask.

"It's simple math, Jack. Do this: make a reservation at a hotel near Times Square. Actually, fuck it. I'll make a reservation. Put your own damn credit card down at the desk when you arrive, though. This goes on your dime."

"What?"

"Tell me you heard me. Millennium Hotel."

I had to shake my head to catch up. Then my eyes landed on the pairs of sneakers I'd taken from Mody's place in Tiburon. In the bottom of my closet: the Barkleys, the Air Max 95s and the Jordan Elevens. Something stirred inside me. Whether it was for a new pair in my own size or something bigger, maybe the whole enchilada—whatever the Maltese Jordans might lead to. I was ready to go all in. If Gina was leading, I could follow.

"Okay," I said. "You want in, you got it. But expect things to get dirty."

She laughed again. "Don't worry, Jack. This girl cleans up good."

Then she was gone. I put my boxers into the suitcase next to my T-shirts and stood up to go book a flight online.

37

Chew Toy

I took a cab to the airport for my redeye. I wore my best pair of sneakers, the ones I thought had a chance of impressing collectors. These were my high-top Nike Air Force Ones, in brown leather and canvas, designed by the famous New York hip-hop DJ and self-confessed sneaker addict, Bobbito Garcia. There was a record album design pressed into the leather on the outside of each heel and each tongue had the word "Love" with a record as the "o." My man Bobbito had once also gone by the name "Kool Bob Love."

He'd also written a book called, *Where'd You Get Those? New York City's Sneaker Culture, 1960–1987*. How he could bring that all into one book, I had no idea. I'd only found out about it searching his name on Google that afternoon. Truth was, I hardly knew what the sneakers were, other than the fact that they fit. I'd come into them by chance when a friend in LA brought me to a sneaker shop way back when I was big. I couldn't resist buying *something* at that place, and the Bobbitos were all they'd had in my size. Now they were all I could offer to the world of collectors. They were in good condition, too. As I thought about it, I realized I'd moved them from house to house more times than I'd worn them outside.

The airport security line moved fast, and I slowed it down when I had to do the extra work of taking off my high tops before going through the machine. With the extra eyelets and thick leather straps around the ankles, these Bobbitos were no breeze. Truth be told, they were a little bit clunky. Just my small sacrifice to the world of collectors and sneaker connoisseurs I was about to enter.

On the plane, I tucked myself into my seat, an exit row window that offered little more legroom than a normal one. This trip was on my dime, no Leonardi expense account to rely on, so I was going medium stakes. Such was the life of the once-was. In truth, I didn't mind: I had brought a couple of Ambien along for the ride, and this was the adventure I wanted.

The next day, Friday, was the day before the Con. I'd have some time to find young Leno, but I needed to be on my toes as much as possible. I pushed my little seat back as far as I could, popped the pink pill, and held my eyes closed as long as it took for sleep to come.

I woke before we landed; leave it to the pilot to always wake you with a useless announcement thirty minutes sooner than you need it. I sat there thinking it all through, testing my resolve, letting the relaxing effects of the pill work through my limbs.

Finally, I rose to my feet and headed to the bathroom. I was looking for relief, but found a lot less of it once I saw the gap through the curtains into first class. There, sitting right on the aisle, four feet away from me, was Mahogany herself. At her shoulder, a big black suit full of beef slept soundly. She didn't. I watched her cross one pristine leg over the other, and then she glanced around, saw me, and waved me over. I passed through the curtains into the plush, dim lighting of first class.

She stood up to greet me, leaned in for an air-kiss on my cheek. "Hi, Jack," she said, taking my hands in hers. I got a little dizzy, and it wasn't from the flight.

"Hi," I said. "What's going on?"

She winked. "Just going east for a sight or two. Taking them in, you know."

I should have known then why she was making the trip—and that I wasn't going to like it.

Instead, I just nodded at the beefcake. "Who's he?"

"Just the latest chew toy. You know I've got a soft spot for one-time actors." She traced her finger down the back of my hand. "Anytime you're ready, just say the word." She winked.

The big man made a sound in his sleep, something between a groan and a yawn. She cocked her head toward him. "Getting a little worn around the edges," she said. "So, you know. I might be ready to move on."

She had me stumped for a response to that. I stared, trying to read if she had any idea of where I was going.

"So," I said.

She leveled the response right back at me. "So."

"What's in New York?"

Her smile finally broke then. She clucked her tongue behind her teeth. "Oh, Joe didn't tell you?"

"Tell me what?" I knew the answer even before I spoke the last word.

She grimaced.

"He's out. How did he get away from Leonardi and the police?"

Very nicely, Mahogany folded both hands in front of her. Her lips were sealed, it seemed.

"Really?" I said.

She shrugged. "So we know why *I'm* here, Jack. But what are *you* up to? Care to enlighten?"

"Not really. No thanks."

"It's the shoes. That's your angle, right?"

"Tell me how Mody got away."

"Funny," she said, "I didn't think to even ask."

We both stared at each other. She didn't know about SneakerCon. That was my advantage. But how did she know Mody would be in New York?

"Maybe I'll see you in the terminal," she said. "We could split a cab."

"No thanks," I said. "Chew toys get that smell after a while, you know? I prefer to stay away."

She flitted her hand toward the back of the plane. "Go back to coach, Jack. Torrance won't be friendly when he wakes up." She turned and headed for the first-class bathroom, the one with no line.

I turned and walked back through the curtain, past the small seats, all the way to the back of the airplane where I got in line to use the coach restroom. I didn't mind; sometimes I preferred to stand.

38

Yellow Cabs

When we finally landed, I hung back in my seat until I knew Mahogany and Torrance wouldn't be around. As much as I hated staying in the small area of my window seat, ducking my head while I tried to stand, I dreaded another conversation with her about Mody, Leonardi and what I was doing in New York even more. I checked my phone and saw a text from Gina that she'd already landed. Give her credit: she managed a much faster trip than I. Maybe she'd called me as an afterthought. I started to wonder if she planned her trip to trail the Koloas even before she'd roped me in. After my experiences with Maxine, Jane Gannon and Victoria, it felt right to be wary, even if I knew I should try to let that go. Hazard of the job, perhaps, or the life.

I looked up and saw the plane was clear. Stewards and stewardesses were cleaning the aisles, heading toward me. I grabbed my little roller bag from the overhead and got out of there fast.

No sign of Mahogany and Torrence the Chew Toy in the terminal, so I went directly to the curbside and hailed a cab for Manhattan. For once, I was happy to pay my own way.

Sure enough, it was butt-ass cold in New York, the air still and bitter. I'd brought along my flimsy San Francisco winter jacket that would do me fine as long as I didn't spend more than five minutes outside. I should've planned better, known there would be a wait for most everything here. The cab line took the better part of fifteen minutes, and by the time I was in the back of a yellow taxi, my face was numb. I told the driver the name of my hotel and asked him to turn up the heat.

As we pulled away from the curb, I watched all around and especially behind to see if anyone followed. Maybe I was just being paranoid, but that was okay, too. Mahogany meant competition—for the sneakers, for Mody, and *from* Mody. Not that I was planning to bag M&Ms again. Now that he was on his own, and since I'd already been paid off by Leonardi, then not rehired when Mody got loose, I felt inclined to let him have his run at freedom. Old Meyer Mody was someone else's problem now. Namely, that of Ms. Mahogany.

By the time we were out of the airport terminals' runaround, I settled back into my seat and let my eyes cruise the gray New York skyline.

Maybe I dozed off, but I perked up when I started seeing signs of the City. At the Triborough Bridge, my curiosity about Mody and how he got free was eating at me. I wanted to know more of the story, the parts that I'd missed. I called Leonardi. He picked up right away.

"What do you want, Jack?"

"That's how you answer?"

Like a curse, he spat out "Hello."

"I'm in New York," I said. "Want to offer me a job?"

"Why would I do that?"

I waited him out. Finally, the shuffling of papers or whatever I could hear on his end stopped. "The fuck are you doing there, anyway?"

"I'm here with Mahogany. We're lovers now."

He laughed. "Watch out for that one. She'll bite your balls, eat you like that spider does." An awkward breath passed before either of us spoke again, then he said, "You bring in Mody again, I'll give you the same as before."

"Double, Joe."

He grunted, as close to an agreement as I would get.

"How'd he get away, anyway?"

With the guilt in his voice of a bad husband who'd been caught cheating, he said, "Wasn't me."

I waited. Outside the taxi window, I saw the line for the toll was down to just a few cars.

"That's it?"

"I brought him to trial, got him to the cops, and from there they lost him. He slipped out of the van during transfer. So."

"He slipped the van? How the fuck?"

"What do I care? Not my bag."

"But you want him again. There some kind of reward now? Bond reissue?"

"I don't know why you're there, Jack. But if you want to make yourself useful, I'll pay you. That's all I should have to say."

"Okay, Joe. Thanks for the tip. I'll let you know." I hung up the phone, and it felt good. To say my relationship with Leonardi had soured was an understatement. Now there was something he wasn't telling me; if Mody had gotten away from the cops, then Joe would get his bond back free and clear. He'd have no more reason for involvement. The cops would be after Mody, and if he crossed state lines, it'd become a federal issue.

So, Feds or the family—if Mody's fate was going to end up in the hands of one or the other, then things had gotten much darker for him. That dumb fuck. He just couldn't see himself straight, could he?

I had to admit, though, a part of me was pulling for him, wanted him to get his Maltese Jordans back and find the beach again on Kauai. But, if he could do one thing well, it was burn his bridges. In Kauai, he'd wronged the Koloas; in San Francisco, the mob, the police, and Joe Leonardi; now here, in New York, I had no idea who he might piss off. A conference full of sneakerheads? I wouldn't put it past him. How long until he had a cadre of them wanting his blood, I could only wonder.

He didn't care. He had one thing, that Holy Grail of Jordans, driving his whole train.

Maybe a similar part of me, but smaller, is what had brought me to New York City, to this taxicab and the bridge I was now crossing into Manhattan. The tall brick projects of Harlem greeted me from the other side of the river, famous Rucker Park with its sneaker-clad summer league somewhere below them. Beyond these, Manhattan was all tall buildings—money as far as the eye could see. Nothing but money.

My face close to the window, I whispered, "It's gotta be the shoes."

39

Breakfast at Tiffany's

I found the Millennium Hotel in Midtown, dutifully put down my credit card at the desk for incidentals and room charges, and headed up to our room. Somehow, even coming from Hawaii, Gina still beat me there. Maybe she flew over the pole? I had no idea. But I could hear her singing in the bathroom, water splashing, when I got inside the suite.

It wasn't a bad room, normal for New York standards, which meant small. But everything in it was new and plenty for what we needed.

I went into the bedroom and sat on the platform bed and took off my Air Force Ones: first undoing the leather strap, then loosening the laces. I took my socks off, too, let my feet sink into the thick carpet, and gripped it with my toes. After the hours cooped up on the plane, it all felt damned good.

After a while, I let out a sigh, and Gina heard me. "Who is it?" she sang out.

I got up, saw the bathroom door was open and walked right in. I found Gina chin-deep in bubbles, the big tub practically full, her dark hair pinned up on top of her head.

"Naughty, naughty," she said. She raised a dripping toe out

of the bubbles and pointed it at the door. I could see the red polish on her toenails. "Back out, please."

I stood my ground. "How about, 'How was your flight?'"

"Mine was tiring, thanks," she said, "and I absolutely had to get into this tub right away to make myself whole again." I wasn't sure where the whole *Breakfast at Tiffany's* vibe was coming from, but I could respect a woman's right to a private tub.

"Okay." I told her I'd wait in the bedroom, then backed myself out and closed the door. The smell of soap and perfume and rich fruit hung in the air, and I liked that. I realized I was glad that she had come along.

Not long after, I woke up on the bed to Gina straddling me, wearing only her towel. When I tried to sit up and get a look at how far down it came, she pushed me back.

Her lips in a pout, she said, "No peeking."

I tried lifting just my head, but couldn't see anything more than the white hotel towel, wrapped just above her cleavage, and her bare, tanned shoulders, her tanned neck. Her hair was down now, hanging wet around her face.

She leaned over me and began to massage the front of my shoulders. I smelled that soapy fruit scent. I was getting hard and didn't mind if she knew it.

"How was your flight, Jack?"

She wore dark red lipstick, and it gave me ideas. Oh, did I have ideas.

"Flight was tiring," I said. "But I'm good now."

She traced her fingers along my clavicle, started to knead my chest.

"You look good," I said.

"Does that mean you missed me?"

Parts of me did, I knew that much. And I didn't have an interest in using more words.

"Come here," I said, and I pulled her down onto me, kissed away her lipstick and tested the warmth of her neck. By the time I got my hands to her back, the towel started slipping away, and then all I needed to do was get my own clothes off—fast. Luckily, I had help.

40

Sn'eads

We woke up properly in the late afternoon, picked up a late lunch, and then scoped out the convention rooms at the Marriott Marquis in Times Square. They had started setting up for the Con, so most of the space was closed off. A guard stood at the door and wouldn't let us in, but we could see inside behind him. There was a lot of space cordoned off for the show. This thing was going to be big. Giant. And it all started the next morning at nine. The guard said they'd held one of these before and kids had camped out in the hallways to be the first inside.

I knew it was a long shot, but I went down to the front desk to ask if anyone had checked in with the last name Koloa or Mody. No on both counts.

I was out of ideas.

Gina stood next to me in the lobby, surveying the scene. She wore a tight black dress with a notch cut in at the shoulder. The fabric parted clear down to her cleavage, revealing a swath of soft, tan skin that I did my best to keep my hands off.

Across the grand lobby, I saw a series of chairs grouped together, some with tables, some not. Chairs of different sizes and shapes, plants, couches. It was a veritable oasis for lounging and quiet conversations amid Times Square's insanity.

"What's next?" she asked.

"We wait?"

"No way," she said. "Not this girl." She pointed at herself with two thumbs. "I'm getting a drink. Come on."

She led the way, and I followed her to the bar at the other end of the lobby. It was a swanky deal on one side of the main floor, and people felt free to take their drinks anywhere else in the lobby they wanted.

We climbed onto a couple of high leather stools, and Gina ordered a martini. The barkeep looked at me with raised eyebrows as he waited for my order.

"Club soda with lime," I said.

Gina made a face. "You sure?"

"Otherwise I won't ever leave. And maybe I'll miss something important."

"Boring." Gina winked, then changed her order to a Sapphire and tonic. "To pace myself."

I leaned back and watched the flow of guests checking in. Some were clearly tourists, families here on vacation who wanted to stay in the thick of Times Square and Broadway; others were here on business, wearing suits and dragging small roller board suitcases. Then a guy came in from the valet area pushing a full luggage cart stacked high with sneaker boxes—a lot of them Nike, a few displaying the familiar Jordan brand.

Our drinks came.

Another guy came in following the first, pushing another cart with more sneaker boxes. Both of them wore T-shirts and jeans, Jordans and baseball caps.

"Check out these two," I said.

Gina turned around. "Who are they?"

"Sneakerheads. Must be here for the Con."

"What are they wearing?" she asked. "Jordans?"

"Yeah. Jordans." I could see one was wearing some mostly-black Jordans that I didn't recognize. The other had on some Jordan ones, the original. "Those are old school kicks. Definitely 'heads."

I took another sip of my soda and told Gina I'd be right back. I stood up and walked across the lobby to the two guys. One was busy checking in, so I went up to the second guy, the one wearing blue denim ones.

"Excuse me," I said. "Are you two vendors for tomorrow's show?"

"Whoa!" The guy stepped back when he saw me. I noticed his T-shirt read FIEND over the silhouette of a Jordan sneaker. "Jack Palms. Man. Ha!" He grabbed my hand and pumped it. "You here as the talent?"

For a second I didn't know what he meant by talent, then I gathered that shows like SneakerCon might hire actors like myself—has-beens—to add a thin level of stardom to the proceedings. If anyone even cared. My guess was that these people came just for the kicks.

But I didn't know what was worse: that I might actually be *the guy* who'd take money for a conference appearance like this, or that he already presumed I was.

"Dude. Sweet." His partner came over and bumped my fist. His shirt had a big cursive G on it. "Jack Palms, son. What up?"

I couldn't speak, wanted to dig myself into a hole for has-beens and hide in it. Maybe chasing guys like Mody and working for Joe Leonardi wasn't any better. Who's to say?

The first one I'd talked to actually took my hand again, shook it. "I'm Hassan. Call me Haas."

"Word up. They call me Mecca Medina." The second one pointed at my sneakers. "Nice Beef 'N Broccolis too, yo."

"Huh. What?"

"Your Bobbitos. Air Force One Winter Pack, 2007. Them are sick. He called them 'Beef 'N Broccoli.'"

We both shrugged. Then, just like so many other times, my mouth didn't fail. Ever the actor, I smiled, slid into a role, and asked what pairs they were most proud of.

Hassan asked me what my favorite Jordan model was. I didn't hesitate.

"Elevens."

He nodded, started to smile and held up a finger. "Yeah," he said. "Let me show you something."

They had me when Hassan opened a brand new box of mostly black Jordans with some red trim. He moved the tissue away and lifted one out. I held it. They were the same ones I had taken from Mody. My first pick, exactly as I remembered from Jordan's playing days in the '95–'96 season where the Bulls won eighty-two games. These were *the shoes* for me. He had nailed it on his first try.

"Eleven Breds," Mecca said. "Dead stock. That is one beautiful pair of sneakers."

I felt a rush in my blood, knew I was at least in some way hooked and already a part of the festivities. In some part of my being, I was one of them: a sneakerhead.

"These are nice," I said. "Fucking sweet."

"Let you have 'em for $350. Player's price for you, Jack."

I smiled and passed the shoe back. Even if I did want it, this wasn't the time or the place. "No thanks. Not my size." I could see on the box they were size 11.5, the same as Mody's pair, right in the standard range for collectors.

"Okay. Okay. How about these?" Hassan put the Elevens back on the luggage cart and opened another box, this one with a strange but familiar pattern on the cardboard. It kind of looked like an elephant's skin. Inside the box was a brand new pair of Jordans that I knew immediately from my youth.

"White and cement '88 retros, Jack. The Jordan Three. What can I say about these? Just three words: free throw line jam."

"I think that's four words."

"Maybe. Whatever. Still, these were the shoes he wore for that dunk contest. You know 'em. Same model: 1988 free throw line jam. Perfect 50. Picture it. Tell me you can't?"

"I can."

"See that? Money. Check the back. See how it has the original Nike Air and swoosh instead of the Jumpman. This how they originally dropped, '88 Retros. Full throwback."

I said, "That's nice."

Hassan said, "Let you have 'em for $300. Basically giving them to you for that. They your size, too."

I stared at the shoe. Something stirred inside me, I couldn't deny it. "No thanks. Really."

Undeterred, he checked my feet. "You're what, a 14, yo? Email me and I'll hook you up." He slid a card into my hand, put the shoebox back onto the luggage cart.

"Yeah. I'll do that."

Hassan said, "For a big talent like you, I can get you whatever you want. Even these." He showed me the sneakers he was wearing: an all-black pair of Elevens, with a blue silhouette of Jordan on the side. He had pulled up his jeans' leg to show me. "Space Jams. Boom."

"Yeah. I'll do that." I held up the card, thinking that I probably would be contacting them to buy some sneakers one day soon.

They gave me elaborate handshakes, and walked off, pushing their carts.

When I got back to Gina, the waitress was replacing her drink.

"Those guys are the real deal," I said. "Addicts. Freaks. The guy's shirt actually says FIEND."

She looked at me flatline. "Really? Do tell."

I sat back in my chair. "Let me ask you. Why are you really here? If it's just about the money, you're at risk of a major disappointment."

She smiled, leaned forward and touched my hand. "Jack Palms," she said, "is it so hard to imagine I came here to be with you?"

In my twenties I'd have panicked and run. In LA I skated from these proposals like an Olympian; now I just sat still, willing myself in place, letting it soak in. I had come to realize when to shut my mouth; I had earned the patience of age.

I wanted to say something pithy and didn't. I kept my mouth closed.

I saw the benefits of her company, liked them, and knew

enough to *try* not to fuck it up. Without worrying about where Gina would follow me long-term or if either of us would get a big payout on the Jordans, I could handle some fun. Sometimes a man had to grit his teeth and bear a good thing or two. For me, that was a hard lesson to learn.

"And besides," she said, "is it really so hard to imagine that I have some interest in these sneakers, too? I mean, come on, Jack! These are rare Jordans. The most rare! I'm all in."

I raised my glass. "To that, then. All in. Let's have some fun."

We clinked and made solid eye contact—someone once told me it guaranteed good sex.

I sipped the soda and raised my hand for the waitress. It was time to order something with a kick.

41

Red October

Two drinks in, Gina was half on my lap in the lobby, and my plan of watching the new check-ins closely had fallen away. Then I noticed a commotion I couldn't ignore: a crowd had gathered at the front desk; guests squeezing in around someone with a luggage cart. A few security guards stepped up to the fray, wearing gray suits and short-cord earpieces, talking into their wrists. Soon a couple of others appeared to help with the crowd management.

When they'd pushed people back far enough for the center of attention to breathe, I saw a kid in the middle of it all: late teens, maybe twenty, wearing a backwards baseball hat, low-slung jeans shorts that came down to his mid-calf, and funky-looking multicolored Air Force Ones. He had a glass case on his luggage cart. Inside it, from what I could tell, was a single pair of all-red sneakers.

"Hang on," I told Gina. "Let me see what this is about." I displaced her from my lap, stood up, and swayed just a little. I wanted this to be more about the lack of blood flow to my legs from her sitting on them than the drink, but I wasn't fully sure. I took a few breaths.

"Those Yeezies," someone nearby said with excitement, on his way over to the crowd.

Gina said, lightly slurring, "You find out. You're the *inspector*."

I gave her a quick second look, wondered if maybe we were going down a road that would end badly—for the job—and kept going. One thing about her was sure: she kept things interesting.

When I got closer, I asked one of the younger kids in the group, "What are those?" He wore a Mets hat that looked like it had just come out of a box and landed on his head without ever being touched by human hands. It was that pristine. You could calibrate a level on the flatness of its brim.

"Those are Air Yeezy II, Red October. Not fake. Signed. Those big money."

All of a sudden, Hassan and Mecca Medina were right next to me, pushing in closer.

"Damn, yo. That is a *sweet* pair. Those could go for *a lot*. Signed by Kanye, too. Damn!"

All I could see in the box was a pair of sneakers that looked too red, too clunky. They didn't have any other colors. Just red. "*Those*? Those are the Yeezys? They're so… *red*."

"Kanye," Mecca said. "Fucking 'Ye. Those are his last joints with Nike. Dropped in a quick strike, no warning, and sold out in a minute. Nike just released whatever they had in stock. So limited."

Haas said, "Online they start at five grand."

Hot was definitely a word to describe them. I couldn't imagine what you would wear with such red sneakers.

Hassan held up his phone, comparing a picture on it to the

kid with the Yeezys. "That's him," he said.

"Who?"

"The collector. He's from Bayonne, got them signed at the concert last month at Barclay Center. Them shits are a signed pair. Hence the glass case. No touching."

I pushed forward to get a better look. One of the security suits caught my eye. Then he recognized me, winked, but still made a subtle push motion with his hand, telling me to stay back.

The kid who owned them was talking nonstop to anyone who would listen, promoting a website, it sounded like, and talking about the other sneakers on his cart. He kept using the word "booming."

"Business be booming," he said.

Hassan and Mecca moved off to talk with a few others in the crowd about the Yeezy sneakers and what they were worth. I stared at the glass-enclosed kicks for a few heartbeats, felt nothing about them, no pull, and went to ask Mecca more questions.

"Be serious," I said. "What are those worth?"

He turned toward me, smiled. "Shit. I'd *love* to know. Definitely serious money. They were so limited. Barely released because Nike couldn't take any more of his shit."

"But they're kind of ugly, right?"

He laughed, hit Hassan on the shoulder. "I'd rather collect the rare Jordans, OG colorways, but whatever. People now... those shoes are the hottest thing. The Hypebeast working. What can I say?"

"What about history? Ones Jordan wore, sneakers that released back when he was playing?"

A collector in the crowd turned toward us and said, "'Ye a

piece of history, man. My nigga historic. These sold out in eleven minutes when they dropped."

Hassan gestured toward this guy with a thumb. "See? Nike had to dump them in the night but that just made them more expensive, sought-after. Supply and demand."

Another guy chimed in with, "Adidas *the brand* anyway because they the original dope shit. Originals. Forums, Shell toes, Run DMC. All that."

Another kid, this one wearing a Kangol bell top over his eyes, said, "Jordans the only. The bomb. They the apex."

Someone else said, "Say word."

Kangol said, "Word, son."

"Word."

I stood where I was, letting it all wash over me. There was more to this I wanted to understand. Especially if I needed to find a market for the Maltese.

I said, "These Octobers are so expensive because there are such a limited quantity. Not just because they're red."

Mecca said, "Exactly. That's simple economics."

The kid from Bayonne finished checking in, and the guards cleared a path for him to walk to the elevators. He pushed the luggage cart with the glass case on it himself. Some of the crowd followed him, but the rest started breaking up, heading to the bar and other parts of the lobby.

A guard said, "That's it. Show's over."

I waved over to where Gina was sitting, asked Mecca and Hassan if I could buy them a drink. Hassan had been about to walk over to the bar, but now they both stopped, turning to me like I was about to make an illicit proposal. I guess that was the downside of being associated with LA.

I said, "I'd just like to ask you a few questions. My girlfriend and I have an interest in a particular pair of shoes."

They both looked at each other and back at me, then shrugged. "Bet," Mecca said.

I led them over to Gina and pulled two more chairs around our little table. The big leather chairs slid easily on the shiny floor. They each looked from myself to Gina, sized her up from her ankles to her eyes and raised their eyebrows as if to say they'd happily go right upstairs with her, if she was into that.

She wasn't.

Hassan waved over a waitress as they looked over the small, leather bar menu. He said, "What you want to buy us with that movie money, Jack?"

Gina shot me a look and leaned an ear toward her shoulder. She didn't trust these two. That was clear.

"Whatever you want." I said, "Listen, have you ever heard of a collector called M&Ms?"

Their faces went sour. "Eminem?" Mecca said. "Who hasn't heard of Eminem. What the fuck."

"No." I shook it off—they meant the rapper. "His friends call him M&M like the candy. His name is Meyer Mody? Some people call him Sneakers or Shoes? He's from Hawaii."

"Hawaii?" Mecca shook his head. "Don't know nobody in Hawaii collect, man."

The waitress came over, and they each ordered an 18-year-old single-malt scotch—sure to be kick-ass stuff and cost more than $20 a glass, especially here in New York City.

I tried a wider approach. "I heard there might be a pair of

Jordans at this show, special ones my friend told me about. I want to know if they're real."

"He wants a pair of Jordans, any pair, they'll be here."

I said, "Have you ever heard of a pair called the Maltese Jordans?"

Hassan and Mecca exchanged a look.

"You serious? For real?"

I nodded. And when I did, their whole demeanors changed. Gone was the suspicious-of-LA-actors-and-freaky-sex vibe; now they both leaned in to listen closely, actually rubbing their hands.

Mecca said, "Say what now?"

42

The Maltese

Hassan squinted at me. "Did you just say the *Maltese*?"

"That's what I said."

Mecca shook his head. "Ghost pair, bro. Hardly heard of, never seen. Them some sneaky-type legendary shits."

I said, "I've seen them."

The waitress brought our drinks, and the guys waited for her to leave before either of them spoke.

Then Mecca leaned closer. "You saw the video."

"No," I said, "I saw the pair. I was in a room with them."

"Huh-uh." Hassan shook his head. "Those part-myth, part-legend. You? *You saw* them?"

"I did. I was—" I held my hand at arm's length. "They were right there."

Mecca checked around the lobby to be sure we no one could hear. "I had no idea," he said. "You said they're coming here?"

Gina gave me another look, reached forward to touch my knee. I knew she was worried that I shouldn't be telling these two what we knew, but I was too far into it, rolling too much with the drinks to stop now.

"They might be. I don't know. I'm looking for some

background on them. Trying to get a sense of what they could be worth."

"I know the shoes you're talking about," Mecca said. "I like to call them the Saudi Set."

Hassan nodded, as if he were giving permission to go on.

"I've seen the videos, read the rumors on the message boards. It's really all about Saudi Arabia and the king, isn't it? The story behind."

Hassan said, "Malta's not where you'd expect to find that kind of money, you know. Being such a small island. But the name's cool. Like the book or something. Still, that game, it was played for the Saudi king."

I nodded. "I know. I saw the video, too."

Mecca said, "They're real," and then he sat back like this confirmed something he had wondered about for a long time. Neither of them spoke for a while, so I sipped my drink, waited.

Gina said, "Jack, what about that dinner we had planned with our friend?"

I shook my head. Maybe there was danger in letting these two know what we'd seen, but they had information for us, too.

I said, "It's cancelled. This is why we're here."

She looked unsure, but I decided to focus on Mecca and Hassan.

"What do you think those would be worth?" I asked. "Any idea?"

Finally, Hassan said, "I'd take out a loan on my house for those. Damn. They might cost more than my house."

Mecca said, "Shit, both our houses. There's no telling what you could get for those." He rubbed his hands together. Then he got real serious, Gary-Coleman-what-you-talkin-bout-Willis serious. He stared me down. "Who's your friend? Where'd you see them?"

"M&Ms," I said. "Meyer Mody, like I told you. I was just there in Kauai."

"Where is he now? Does he have them?"

I opened my hands. "He had them. Now they're with someone else."

"Who?"

I winced. "They've passed into the hands of a business partner he had to take on."

Mecca whistled and smiled. "If you knew how to get them, or who had them, we could help you broker a deal. *Definitely.* We'll help you find the right buyer. And that shit ain't easy."

Something conspiratorial passed between the two collectors. They finally turned to their glasses and raised them. We all toasted our drinks. Gina shot me another look and brushed her hair back behind her ear. As they each took a long pull of scotch, she shook her head just the slightest bit.

When they set their drinks down, they both sucked their teeth and smiled in approval.

Mecca said, "Now tell me: are they really coming to this Con?"

"I think they are."

Without waiting a moment, Mecca said, "Bring them to us first. We'll get your friend as good an offer as he's going to get."

I checked Gina's face: stone cold.

"How much?" I asked.

Mecca waved the question away. "You seem like nice enough

people. You care? You want to know the story?"

"Yeah," I said. "I want the full deal. You tell us about these Jordans, and I'll buy you another round of anything you want to drink."

Mecca nodded. Hassan rubbed his hands together. He was puffing up a little at the thought of this pair.

Mecca took another sip, then leaned toward us to speak softly.

43

Full Story

"So you know how the Saudis got their money," Mecca said. "Oil. They've always had it. They hope they always will. I'm talking about more money than they know what to do with. These are the money men with the *ghutra*, the robes, all of it. They are the reason the word money was invented."

"What?" Gina asked.

"Kidding," he said, "kidding." He waved it off.

Hassan added, "And they can still play ball, yo. No dizza. Well, some of them anyway."

I checked the rest of the lobby quickly, monitoring the front desk out of the corner of my eye.

Mecca said, "Let's start in 1996. Just after Jordan's fourth finals. Ring four. He's back from retirement number one, just had the best year of his life on the court. Historic fucking proportions. The Bulls just posted the league's best record *ever*. Seventy-two wins. Nobody ever broke seventy wins before that.

"We pick up that summer. Jordan plays a big, high-stakes golf game and loses. He winds up with a debt. Big one. Who's the man he owes? Well, he's just lost this bet to Donald Trump. Trump himself. The original Don. Asshole, headpiece combover."

Hassan spit out a few curse words, followed by, "Trump. This is the guy who won't leave Obama alone about his birth certificate, demands proof that a black man wasn't born in Africa."

Mecca shakes his head. "Motherfucker." He takes a few breaths. "Anyway, Jordan plays Pebble Beach after the 1996 NBA Finals and makes a million-dollar bet. To a normal person this is a shitload of money. Even to Jordan, it's nothing to sneeze over. But he's a gambler and Trump is a *nasty* businessman; nasty enough to raise the stakes and keep going. What do you know? He's also a damned good golfer. What else does he have to do with his time back then? No *Apprentice* or nothing.

"And Jordan? Despite what you may have heard, he wasn't that good a golfer. So Trump whups him up and down the fine pebbles of the beach all morning. Freaking Trumps his shit, literally. All day long. For thirty-six holes. By the time they're done, His Airness has doubled down and re-bet enough times that he's deep into the Don for close to fifteen now."

"Fifteen what?"

Mecca grimaced like it pained him to explain, then made an M with his fingers so we were sure to know the denomination.

Gina sat far back in her chair, noncommittal. If I read her reaction right, it was part *How could it be that much?* and part *How the fuck could this happen?*

Mecca paused and turned to Hassan.

"Come on," I said. "Spill."

Hassan started in, his voice lowered. "You're not seeing the full picture. This has way bigger implications than just money, yo. To get to why, we have to go back a few years. Check it.

"This is the part you may have already heard: it's that Jordan's whole career was in jeopardy. On the court because of what he did off it. The possibility of no more Jordan." He shook his head as if it was too horrible to continue. "No second coming, no return from baseball."

Mecca took over. "Look, 1992 is when the gambling allegations start coming in against him. Jordan had to testify in a federal case against a cocaine dealer named Slim Bouler about why this dirtbag had a check signed by MJ for fifty-seven grand. Turns out he says it's from one day's poker losses." He sipped his scotch. "And dude, this freaks the commissioner the fuck out. David Stern, high commissioner, gets his skivvies *all* up in a bunch.

"Don't forget, this just a couple years after all of baseball had to weather the fucked up storm of the Pete Rose scandal. His gambling. Remember how ugly that got? Dude still not in the Hall of Fame."

As a kid who followed sports, I remembered the Pete Rose scandal. It had been a major event, like the excommunication of the sport's high bishop.

"David Stern sure as shit didn't want that. Fuck no. Michael Jordan and any implication of betting on games? Oh, man. That could've destroyed the league. Then a couple of other things pop up linking MJ to the mob and gambling. Cracks in the armor like a motherfucker. He drops a million cash to Dick Esquinas in '93, gets caught playing baccarat all night in Atlantic City during the '93 conference finals against the Knicks."

Hassan slapped his own knee. "At the casino all night. With a game that next day!"

Mecca shook it off. "Jordan super-competitive, as you know. Can't stop himself anytime, for anything. This addict in him is part of what made him so damned good. The dog instinct. But gambling? That's a problem. His father turns up dead that summer of '93, people start linking *that* to gambling, saying the mob trying to scare him to pay his debts, and it starts looking bad for our man.

"Think that didn't scare the Angel of Stern? MJ starting to look like Pete Rose. Whole league could get fucked. MJ one bad bet away from going extinct. Stern goes on high alert.

"That summer, there's an investigation by the league. It starts right after the '93 finals. Then guess what? Four months later, Jordan goes away. Retires. He says from burning out. Needs a break. Come on. This guy *loves* basketball like nothing else. His calling."

Hassan couldn't resist chiming in. "Baseball? Bullshit. You think that was his idea? Come on. He does not leave the game he loves. Not if there wasn't something else in play."

Mecca said, "In his retirement speech, Jordan says some cryptic shit." He held up air quote fingers to let us know he was reciting from memory. "He says, 'If David Stern lets me back in the league,' when they asked if he might come back."

I had to ask, "Where's this all coming from? Where did you get this?"

"This is truth. Facts. You got to educate yourself, Jack."

Hassan added, "Call it a conspiracy theory. Whatever you want. It's out there. Look it up."

I leaned back, turned to Gina, got nothing, then took a deep breath. "Fine," I said. "What next?"

"Jordan goes away for a couple of years, they drop the investigation, everyone's better off."

None of this had anything to do with the sneakers, so far as I could see. I would have mentioned that, but they were preaching to my choir, talking old-school hoops. I could have listened to them go on all day.

As if he'd read my mind, Mecca finished his drink, said, "But back to the sneakers. Now you've got a twice-shy Jordan dropping big money gambling to the Don in '96. The fuck was he thinking?"

Hassan held up his glass. "Seriously. And can we get another round of these?"

I waved to the waitress.

Mecca kept right on talking. "He's thinking if Stern finds out about this, he's done. *Done.* So it's not just Juanita he has to hide this money draw from, it's the whole world: the press, the NBA, David Stern, everybody. He's just won title *four* after a 72–10 season. He *knows* he got more run left in him. *Much more.* And so what is His Airness to do?"

Hassan holds his hands out, palms open. "This is where it gets crazy."

"His career in the balance," I said. "So what's he do?"

Gina had her elbows on her knees, stretched forward with a drink in her hand. She swirled around what was left of it: mostly ice, a straw, and a lime. She had been following it all, barely touching her drink. I started to believe she might finally be that unicorn: a woman who could talk old-school basketball and care, not check out after two minutes; a woman who knew the details of Michael Jordan's career and thought they mattered.

231

"You okay?" I asked her.

She smiled. "I used to watch those games with my dad growing up. I loved the Bulls."

The waitress brought the second round of 18 year, and I told her I'd have one myself. I wasn't going anywhere, and I couldn't resist. As fast as she rushed back to the bar to get it, I started to wonder if these weren't maybe thirty-dollar glasses we were drinking.

"So what'd he do?"

They drank for a moment. Gina sipped hers through a straw.

Mecca got back to it: "His one ace in the hole? The man who *maybe* had more money to lose than Jordan himself on this whole debacle: Phil Knight. The Nike Godfather himself. That's who Jordan turned to."

"Nike." It was all I could say.

"Knight has the money to bail his man out, but there's no way he can make that kind of withdrawal unnoticed, either. Not on the business books. Plus, Stern would be watching. But Knight was connected."

Hassan raised his glass and then his eyebrows. "He had a friend. A sheik."

Mecca said, "King Fahd, is one old-school, freaky, funky sneakerhead. A collector well before any of us were considering it. Dude liked his things shiny, you follow? Air Jordans. Gold. And Phil Knight knew it."

Hassan said, "Think he didn't want some fly kicks under that kaftan? He loved him some fresh Air Max to flow across his Persian rugs. And know what else? Sheik was a *huge* hoops fan. *Loves* to watch the Americans ball."

Mecca nodded. "Plus, dude had enough money to buy and sell Nike. We're talking Saudi-oil-money pull. Buy all of Beaverton."

"There you go," Hassan said. "King Fahd is like where the word pull even comes from."

"What?"

Mecca stopped for a second, looked to Hassan and smiled. "Yep."

Hassan waved it off. "That's right. What we talking."

Animated, Mecca waved his arm, spitting out more of the story as fast as he could. "They all go. Jordan, Tinker, and Phil Knight himself. Everyone but the cartoon characters from *Space Jam*. They play one game. Quarters, running clock, Humpty Dumpty and all the king's men against Jordan and team nobody.

"They take the pictures we've seen, the video. King has Kareem, the Captain, God Shammgod, Moses Malone, any deity name or Muslim motherfucker he can find. Mahmoud Abdul-Rauf shooting threes like the Tourette's patient you know he is. Doesn't matter. Jordan dusts them all. Some say even Wilt Chamberlain was there. But I don't think so."

Hassan's hands shook as he said, "Game is crazy, too. Dudes putting up buckets like they raining from Saudi oil fires. King's team goes for like 97 points, and Jordan scores 110 *himself*. Bananas-type game. Niggas just *ballin'*. This action is *fan-freaking-tastic*."

Mecca waited for his partner to wind down. "And when it's all over," he said, "they take the pictures we've all seen, leave the signed shoes as a keepsake memento of the whole experience for the king, and that's a wrap. Jordan goes home, pays off the

Donald, goes back to playing and wins two more titles in rapid succession. Never looks back, no one's the wiser, and it's all said and done."

"But the sneakers remain!" Hassan threw his hands up. "These ones. The stuff of legend. Boom. And you say you actually saw them with you own eyes? Damn! Do you know what I'd pay just to *hold* those?

I nodded, closed my eyes in respect.

Mecca said, "That is the story of the Maltese."

44

The Saudi Set

"Wow." My mouth was dry from the story, though I hadn't spoken in a while. The waitress brought my drink and put it in my hand. I tasted the 18-year scotch. It was smoky and bitter, better than I had imagined. Who cared about price?

Mecca said, "You see why I call them the Saudi Set."

Hassan broke in, "And that's what's so crazy, yo: that the king ever let these shoes out of his possession."

Mecca shook his head. "Fahd got sick, things started to fall to pieces around 2003, and then Abdullah doesn't give a shit about the Jordans. Think he's worried about his half-brother's stupid sneakers? Not at all. All of it goes out in an estate sale of epic proportions. Scattered to the four corners with nobody keeping track of any of the good shit. For all we know, dudes were running the dunes in yellow satin, jewel-studded Air Max with no regard."

"Can you imagine what might have been in there? We'll never know."

I checked Gina, made sure she wasn't about to give a smart-ass answer. To my relief, she didn't.

"In any case, all we know next is that the Saudi Jordans come into the possession of someone in Paris around 2006. This is someone smart, private *and* interested in a major buy-and-hold strategy. He knew the history. From there they drop out of circulation and awareness completely. That is, until your buddy somehow shows up with them in Hawaii. *That* is a story I'd like to know: how your friend got his hands on these."

Hassan said, "How the fuck *did* your friend get his hands on these?"

"I don't know."

"What was he going to do with them?"

I held up my hands. "What do I know? He's a collector, an addict. What do any of you do with these things?"

Mecca Medina, who was wearing a pair of Jordans I had seen on eBay for over $600, said, "Not wear them. Not the Maltese."

Gina screwed up her face. "But from Paris? What would he be doing over there?"

I shrugged. "Maybe the sneakers came to him." I had no clue. I said, "I almost had them in my hands."

There was a period of time when no one said anything. Call it a silent moment of appreciation over the magnitude of my statement.

Mecca said, "Almost?"

"Yo, my man. Tell me there was like a fence between you and those kicks. Like something very immovable stopping you from touching them."

I said, "There was: about a thousand pounds of ill-tempered Hawaiians. Four brothers who would not go easily."

Mecca just shook his head.

Finally, Gina said, "Are they the real Maltese Jordans? Could

Mody have actually had them?"

Mecca was deep into a train of thought; he barely noticed Gina's question. "Think about what these would prove if you— *or we*—had them?"

Hassan was nodding emphatically. "We heard they were in Hawaii. Let's say those were them. You saw these actual shoes, with Jordan's signature…" Here he exchanged a glance with his partner. "Wouldn't be too hard to confirm if the signature was real. Especially Tinker's. Not a lot of forgeries of that, I bet."

"They had some kind of signature confirmation with them," I said. "A certificate."

"Shit," Mecca said. "These could turn the whole basketball world upside down. Think what the league might pay to keep this quiet. The idea of a backdoor deal between Jordan and Stern about the first retirement? If Jordan was that afraid of a second investigation that he went all the way to Saudi Arabia to play—"

Hassan spat out, "And the fucking Donald of Dons, King Orange Lizard himself, was to blame!"

That's when the dollar signs started dancing in front of my eyes. "What would the Hall of Fame pay for those?"

"Hall of Fame?"

They both shook their heads.

"Fuck the Hall of Fame," Hassan said. "Wrong buyer to be thinking about."

"What about the NBA, Stern, Phil Knight even?" Mecca tapped the table in the middle of us all with his finger. "What would they pay to keep the Hall of Fame from *not* getting those? Here in New York, right up the street from the league offices? Man, we can find some *major* buyers."

Gina's eyebrows went all the way up her forehead. "How much?"

Mecca said, "You're asking my estimate?" They shared a look. "Five million."

"Minimum."

Gina swore. She sat back hard in her chair and swallowed the remainder of her drink, then chewed and spat out the rind of a lime. She laughed at herself.

I waved to the waitress for another round.

"That's a fucklot more than Mody was expecting," I said. Then I thought about how he'd been so willing to cut me in for a half of his original one hundred, how he'd been so eager to run despite long odds at the airport, and how he'd ultimately risked being hunted by the Feds and the San Francisco family to get here and get the shoes back. "Unless, of course…"

And of course he'd never be able to get what he could for the Jordans on Kauai, not compared to what he could get in New York City.

I said to Gina, "That's a lot more than the Koloas think they're worth."

Hassan stood up. His glass was empty and so was Mecca's. "So, what we're saying is if you can get your hands on these shoes, get in touch with us. We'll get you in touch with the right buyers. We can *definitely* help you broker this deal." He slid his card into my hand, showing me a phone number written by hand on the back. "My cell," he said. "You call me *any* time."

Mecca gave me another card. "And mine. In case you can't get him."

"We're here in this hotel."

"And we're *serious*. You *do not* want to do this thing on your own."

They both nodded and started to walk away, still facing us, still talking, telling us how important it was for us to call. I waved the business cards, saying I'd be in touch. Finally, almost at the elevators, they turned and went on their way.

"Oh my God," Gina said. "Can you believe that?"

"I do," I said.

"We're going to be rich!" She did her best to keep her voice down, but I still worried the whole lobby had heard.

45

Leno

"First we have to find them," I said. "And get them away from the Koloas."

"There's our start." She pointed past me. "He's right there."

I turned to look across the lobby: past a series of leather armchairs, potted trees, beyond the opposite side of the bar, all the way to the 45th Street entrance. There I noticed something exciting: Koloa brother number four, Leno.

"There he is," I said, sliding down in my chair.

She asked, "The youngest?"

"That's right. That's him."

"What's he doing here?"

"Same as us," I said. "Looking for a deal. Or information."

Leno walked over to the bar then stood there as if waiting. He was just a few stools over from some of the collectors I had eavesdropped on when the Yeezy Red Octobers arrived.

I watched. Was he here to meet Mody? Or did he even know that Mody was back in play, moving on his own here in New York City?

Then Leno waved at someone. He started over to a man sitting alone at a table, wearing dark glasses and a shiny suit. Two more suits in sleek sunglasses sat at the next table over. The first guy would be the money. And the other two would be the muscle.

Leno took both of the money man's hands in his own. They shook, and he sat down.

"Think they're going to trade right here?" Gina said.

"Where are the Jordans? He wouldn't bring them here."

She leaned closer to me, and I could smell her perfume, the lilac scent of her shampoo. "But he's got them somewhere, right?"

"I'm thinking he'd stash them somewhere close by. Where he could get to them once the money was clear."

She sat forward. "Maybe they're in those planters." She pointed at a stand of ficus trees by the windows.

"Doubtful. Maybe he's got a room upstairs."

Leno talked to Money; Money talked to Leno. They went back and forth a few times, haggling or bargaining, or just shooting the shit, feeling each other out.

"We watch them, follow to where they make a trade," I said.

"But how did he find a buyer before the Con?"

"What's he know about buyers at all?"

Gina laughed. "Fuck, Jack. It's the whole point of this convention. How hard can that be?"

"For a couple of million dollars? Come on. These clowns can't swing that." I pointed to the other collectors and heads around us.

"This is a sneaker conference, Jack. People who buy and sell things at conferences are every bit about the haggle. The hustle."

"Maybe, but those suits aren't your usual conference types."

Now she put her hand on my arm in a soft way, gently stroking it. "Well, look at it as part of the hunt, the story, the chase of it all. That's the fun part of why we're here."

She was right. I squeezed her hand.

"That, and I like money." She laughed, then put her hand over her mouth. I liked that. I liked it a lot.

Leno and the suits stood up. He and Money started walking toward the 45th Street doors with the others right behind them.

"Come on," I said, standing up. "We got to follow them."

Gina hopped up. "Maybe I should just stay here, be sure they don't circle back."

"No way, babe." I grabbed her hand, pulled her along with me. In a moment, she was right by my side, pushing ahead and giggling a little. We were getting into the fun. As we made the revolving doors, she jumped ahead and rushed in before me.

"Come on, Palms. Keep up now."

I shook my head going through the door. Leno and Money stood outside on the corner, flanked by the two suits. They could have been about to hail a cab or just waiting for the light to turn so they could cross. I hoped for the second. Anything like jumping into a cab and saying, "Follow that car," was not what I wanted.

Then they started to cross Times Square, first Broadway and then 7th, staying on 45th at the other side. We stayed about ten or fifteen feet behind, though it was easy to stay lost in the crowds. Times Square at this time of day was lousy with tourists—especially on a Friday.

The day was one of those unseasonably warm ones that pop up in a New York winter every now and again. I was getting by with just a San Francisco jacket, my face unscathed by the chilly wind. Under the full cover of an overcast sky, something of an April warmth had been trapped inside the city's bubble.

We followed them along 45th and away from the crowds, more or less—crowds being a relative term in Midtown. Across 6th Avenue, we watched them go to the north side of 45th Street where the others trailed Leno into the small entrance of a hotel called, conveniently enough, The Hotel @ Times Square. Someone had made the @ in the name look like an apple by adding an accent to its top, like a leaf. Clever, I thought.

The entranceway was just a small, gated door in the street under a black awning with the hotel's name. If we were on the East Side, this could have passed for any of hundreds of doorman-stationed apartment buildings. After the first two stories in concrete, the hotel turned to a nicer brick above them, with bay windows jutting out in threes. Far above us, the building turned concrete again for the penthouse, one that had its own balcony, complete with fancy Greek columns.

I pointed up. "Think they're headed to the penthouse?"

Gina said, "Damned if I know. And damned if I can't find out." She primped her shoulder-length hair with the palm of her hand and walked across the street to the hotel entrance. I followed a few steps behind.

"Make sure they're not in the..." I had meant to warn her about walking in on them in the lobby, but it didn't matter: she wasn't listening and I remembered halfway through that the Koloas had no idea she was a part of this, so far as I knew. If they even remembered her from the island. The Koloas were the type to be remembered by people more than to remember people they met.

I hung back, keeping outside the door in case they were still in the lobby, standing off to the side, facing the street. A white cube truck passed us headed east. My biggest fear now was that Leno would sell the Jordans for far less than they were worth. Shit, if I were him, I'd be fine with six figures for a pair of kicks, even low six figures, like one hundred thousand. That had seemed like a ridiculous sum up until the last hour. Now I thought we could get into the millions and, whether I believed it or not, I wanted to be sure we didn't leave big money on the table.

As I thought about it, my mission became simple and clear: without Mody around, I had to reach out to the Koloas to stop any sale before they knew what they might actually get from the sneakers. If they slipped completely through my hands, I'd never forgive myself. Nor would I get a chance to negotiate for their sale if Leno had already made a trade with Money.

I turned back into the hotel entrance, bumped right into Gina coming out. She pushed me onto the sidewalk.

"They're in the penthouse," she said, fake-fluffing her hair once more. "Feminine wiles triumph again."

"Nicely done." I offered her a fist bump, but she missed seeing it completely. I walked around her and opened the hotel door.

She went right back in, smiling at me as she went. "What's the plan, my man?"

"Simple," I said. "We got to stop that deal."

46

Penthouse Play

The hotel desk clerk wasn't too happy about letting me onto the penthouse elevator at first, exclusive as it was, but a fifty changed that. Two things I was realizing about the Hotel @ Times Square: they were dead serious about the apple motif—the signature fruit was everywhere you looked in the lobby—and it was modest enough that a Koloa brother could afford the penthouse and a fifty could get me right up. Close to Times Square or not, money really could buy you anything in New York, and contrary to popular opinion, your desires didn't always cost so much once you started throwing around the green.

Then again, having Gina by my side didn't hurt, either.

We got onto the exclusive elevator, pressed the top floor button, and we were on our way.

"Penthouse C," Gina said. "That's where they'll be."

"Got it." My hands felt clammy, from the drinking or the nerves, I didn't know.

In a minute, the elevator doors opened, not right onto a penthouse interior, but onto an open, carpeted space with three identical white doors; the top floor of the hotel was divided into just three rooms, all of their doors before us. We headed for the one on the far right, the one marked with a golden *C*.

"What are you gonna do?"

I started knocking. "Leno. Open up!"

Gina took a step back. "Oh. That."

"It's Jack. I've got to talk to you." I pounded on the door.

When the door opened, I was face to faces with the two security suits and Koloa Brother number two, nobody smiling.

"What?" one of the suits said.

Eddie asked, "The fuck you doing here?"

"Don't make this deal."

Gina laughed behind me. "You're just diving right in there."

"What deal?" Eddie said.

I stepped back. "Really? We just followed your little brother from the Marriott. You saying he's not about to sell the Maltese Jordans to these guys?"

Gina stood next to me, hands on hips. "Come on," she said.

All three men turned their heads towards Gina. Eddie asked the question on their minds. "Who the fuck is she?"

"Let me talk to Leno," I said.

Both suits stood in the doorframe, filling it from one side to the other. They crossed their arms, faces full of contempt.

Eddie was gone, headed back down the hall.

"Who the hell is it?" Leno's voice calling from inside the suite.

"Let me in." I tried walking through the suits, but they didn't part. Instead, they poked my chest, pushing me back. Even their fingers felt strong.

"Okay." I help up my hands. "I come in peace."

Now the two suits stepped out into the hall, backing me away.

Gina said, "Guys. Guys. Can't we talk this out?"

As the door started to close, I called out, "They're lowballing you!"

"Fuck off," Eddie called from inside. The door slammed shut.

"What's his offer?" I asked the suits.

Nobody said anything.

Then one of them said, "You two should leave now." He had close-shaved hair and his neck squeezed up out of his collar. His body stretched the fabric of the suit, especially across his shoulders. I figured I could get by him, if I fought dirty, but I wouldn't get past number two.

"What's your man's offer on the kicks?" I asked.

No answer again. Instead, they drew small semi-automatic pistols out of their jackets. They held them downward, not pointing at us. Not just yet, anyway.

"Is that really necessary?" I kept both hands visible.

Gina spoke up. "You two really don't talk much. That right? Want me to put some sexy on you?"

His brow wrinkled, but that was all.

We stood about four feet from the guards and the door: close enough that we could reach them, but far enough that they'd have time to hit us with their guns, or worse.

I turned to Gina. "Looks like he doesn't want to talk to us."

"No, apparently not. How about I kick him in the balls?"

"That sounds all right," I said. "Think you can do it fast enough so he doesn't shoot you?"

Gina checked her distances and bounced back and forth on her toes. The suit was eyeing her; she had his full attention. He lifted the gun.

"Don't even think it."

"He speaks!" I threw my hands up. "It's a miracle."

"Just get in the elevator and fuck off."

The other suit stepped up next to his partner. Now they both had their guns pointed at us.

"You two have a license for those?" I asked. "Wouldn't want to end up like Plaxico, you know. This is New York City, after all."

Their expressions didn't change. I began to think it was really time for us to go.

Then the door to the penthouse suite opened behind the suits. Leno excused his way past them and walked out to meet us. He didn't look happy.

"I don't have any idea what the fuck you're doing here, but you've got ten seconds. I'll give you that on former-celebrity status, alone."

"What's his offer? If it's anything less than a couple million, he's killing you. Do you know what these shoes are worth?"

He pointed toward the elevators. "Enough."

I turned toward Gina and put my arm around her. We both stepped away.

"We're going," I said, over my shoulder. I led her back to the elevator bays and pushed the call button. "See?" I held my hands up for good measure.

"Hang on a second." Leno came closer, stepped right up next to us and said deep under his breath, in a whisper so soft I could barely hear, "What do you know?"

"I mean— We're leaving. Sorry for wasting your time."

He hissed, "Just tell me."

I shrugged. "David Stern, scandal, corruption. The basics. Should I go on?"

Leno nodded. I couldn't tell if this was something new to him or something he already knew. "Where's Mody?" he asked.

"Mody? What do you mean? He's in jail."

The elevator doors opened, and Leno basically pushed us inside, backed by the two suits with their guns raised.

"Did you hear from Mody?" I asked.

Leno stayed put outside the elevator, folded his arms across his chest. He wasn't talking.

Gina and I stared at the three of them as the elevator doors began to close.

"Okay," Gina said. "With that, then."

She held her hands up, and I did the same. The doors closed.

47

Bodega

On the way down in the elevator, Gina said, "That was all you could do?" She hit my arm.

"Yes. Two guns in my face pretty much tears it."

"I see," she said. "My hero." She hit me again.

The elevator doors opened at the lobby, and I steered us out of the car, the lobby and the hotel altogether.

When we were on the street, Gina said, "Fucking Koloas. Excuse my French."

"Excused."

"So what's our play?"

"Simple. We wait and see if the buy happens. If Mr. Money comes out with the shoes, we tail him to his buyer. Then we see what's up." I pointed across the street to a bodega with a few tall chairs inside along the window. "Buy you a coffee?"

"I never say no to coffee."

We went across the street, into the bodega, and ordered two coffees at the deli counter. They came out in little blue paper cups that read WE ARE HAPPY TO SERVE YOU on them. Then we sat in the front window on high stools, letting the coffees' steam warm our noses. I took mine black. I just wanted it hot, and after the double scotch indulgence, I didn't deserve sugar and milk to make it taste good. I needed to be back on my toes.

Gina added cream and sugar without guilt, even asked me if I were carrying a flask to spike the brew. I wanted her on her game, but what did I know about how she operated? So far, she was holding her own. Whatever came next, if it involved tailing multiple people, I might well need a partner in the game, tipsy or clear-eyed.

I put my hand on her back, felt the goosebumps on her skin, and realized she must be cold. So I took off my jacket and draped it over her shoulders. "Sorry I didn't offer sooner," I said.

"It's okay. Thanks."

"I'm glad you're here."

She smiled then, seemed content to stare out the window holding her cup. We'd seen and heard a lot. Maybe she just needed to breathe.

After a while, she said, "So what makes you think this guy isn't the actual buyer? Or that these guys come back out the front and we manage to tail them to wherever they're going?"

I shrugged. "Don't know. But we sit and wait, follow the suits no matter where they go. What's our choice other than that?"

She rubbed my arm. "Well…"

"Plus, I have a feeling in my gut."

"Your gut? Really?" She laughed. "Then I'm satisfied."

Through the front windows of the hotel, I saw the suits step out of the elevator. Just Money and his boys. No Koloas.

"Check it out," I said. "Be ready."

She leaned toward the glass. "Does he have anything?"

I couldn't tell through the hotel windows.

Money said something to the clerk at the desk, and I hoped he wasn't asking him to call a cab. Besides the cliché of it, I flat-out doubted that one cab could really follow another through the sea of yellow vehicles in New York City. What's more, I didn't want to find out.

So I was at the bodega door, ready to move, when the suits exited the Hotel @ Times Square. As I pushed it open, a rush of cold air hit me in the face. I braced against it, and when I looked back across the street, a truck was in my way. I stepped outside, it passed, and I saw them turn left on 45th Street. They were headed back toward 6th Avenue and maybe Times Square.

When Gina came outside, I pulled her to me and kissed her hard on the lips. I liked doing it, but it was also good cover to help us blend in. Just two happy New Yorkers sharing a kiss.

But who was I kidding? We looked like tourists; both of us wore clothes for warmer climates rather than the long, thick coats and hats the locals used against the wind.

The kiss gave us a bit of a trailing position on the three suits, but we started after them. I still couldn't see if they carried anything because of the crowds.

They reached 6th Avenue before us, and again I hoped they wouldn't hail a cab. If they did, 6th would take them uptown, toward Central Park and the Upper West or Upper East sides. Neither of these was a neighborhood I knew well. I'd spent most of my time in the city south of 14th Street, in the Village or various spots below Houston.

It occurred to me this was my first time in New York since my divorce, and that I had never come here clean and sober as an adult. Not that I was clean or sober now. Old patterns, I guess.

Then the light changed and they crossed 6th Avenue, heading back toward Times Square. We kept our distance, and I took Gina's hand.

"Keep me warm," she said. "I'm getting cold like I was back in Minneapolis."

I put my arm around her and clutched her to my side.

"Also, keep me drunk. Wherever we're going. I need another drink."

I laughed. "Maybe we should've brought a flask."

"Yes, obviously."

Up ahead and across the street, I watched Money stop in a storefront and look through the glass. This was the first time I'd had a clear sight of him. I could see his full body and what he held at his waist. There was something there. It was dark—a bag maybe, definitely big enough to hold the shoes.

"Is that it?" she asked.

"Can't tell. It could be. We'll have to get closer to see."

They started moving again, and I pulled Gina by her hand to follow me across the street. Once we reached the north side of 45th, I hurried to make up ground. We were getting close to Times Square, where you could lose anybody in the crowds. I caught a glimpse of Money holding the black bag by his side. He held it under his arm, as if he would protect it with his body if it came to that.

"If those aren't the shoes, I can't imagine what they would be."

"But where are they going?" she asked.

"We'll just have to see."

48

Wayne Embry

It didn't surprise me that the suits took the black bag right back to the Marriott Marquis. If you were going to do anything with a pair of sneakers this rare, SneakerCon was the place. Especially one-of-a-kind Jordan Eleven highs in a unique colorway with a touch of jewels.

When we got back to the lobby, it was buzzing. Anticipation, voices, number of sneakerheads in the room—all the critical numbers were up. The crowd around the bar was three-deep, and if Money and his boys wanted to have their own table, they'd have to wait in line.

Gina and I went through the revolving door together and ducked behind some tall plants. She said, "This place is hopping!"

"Good luck getting a drink."

"Seriously."

We watched Money and his boys stride right past the bar. Then we followed them, first hiding behind another potted plant and then blending into the bar crowd waiting for drinks. I ducked to keep my head from being the highest in the crowd, but I could still see them. I watched Money and his boys keep right on going, directly to the elevators, heading for the higher floors and guest rooms.

"Come on," I took Gina's hand and made the move to follow, hoping to at least get a look at their floor, but I bumped right into a woman who'd moved in front of me. Suddenly she had her hand on my chest.

"Hello, Jack. What's doing?" I looked down, and there was Mahogany, holding a highball in one hand, and chewing on a thin, black straw. "And who's this now?"

Gina looked at me with a little fire in her eyes, something I knew I'd be hearing about, but I didn't want to waste our chance at the suits. I motioned with my head toward where they'd gone.

"On it." Gina let go of my hand, shot Mahogany a twin pair of eye-daggers, and took off through the bar crowd for the far side of the lobby.

"She's a good little one, now. Isn't she?" Mahogany removed her hand from my chest and took the straw out of her teeth. She had chewed it down to a flat nib with her molars, just as I imagined she did to her men.

"Where's your chew toy?"

She smiled and tipped her head, then said on ice, "Torrance is out running an errand. Hunting down a lead."

Mahogany wore a black dress that made Gina's look like it came from an island Quickie Mart. Her look was pure luxury, even down to—I guessed—her heels. The sneakerhead crowd had parted around her, so we had a small oasis of airspace to talk. She had the aura of untouchability, like dirt wouldn't stick to her no matter what.

I craned my neck to see if Gina had gotten to the elevators in time to see where Money and his suits had gotten to, but

Mahogany pulled me back—literally—by taking my chin in her hand and bringing my face, my eyes, back to hers.

"Stick with me, Jack. That girl can wait."

I removed her hand from my face. "Gina," I said. "That's her name."

She talked over me, refusing to register what I'd said. "What's the play, Jack? Where's Mody?"

That she didn't ask about the shoes took me back. I had forgotten about Mody as an item of value. The sneakers were the big catch here and all I cared to find.

"Haven't seen Mody. Is he here?" I tried again to move around her, but she blocked my way. "Listen, I'm on something else right now. No time for this."

"Fine," she said with a pout. She grabbed my wrist then, and I could feel her long, manicured nails digging in. Her face right up to mine, she said, "But Jack, if you find Mody, you bring him to me." She winked. "I'll make it *very* worth your while."

Then she gave my wrist a final dig and let go, headed back toward the bar, going straight for a stool that suddenly became empty in front of her. She didn't look back, and I could feel the chill air in her wake.

Then I moved. I headed around the crowd and toward the elevator banks, checking my wrist for punctures. What I saw there was four new moon crescents in white on my most tender stretch of skin. She'd left her mark. Oh, had she.

I found Gina leaning against the wall in the elevator bay, arms folded and eyes set to sting. "Who's that?" she asked me, as soon as I got close enough.

"That," I said, "is the competition, San Francisco's most feared and successful bounty chaser, Mahogany."

"Mahogany what?"

I shrugged. "Just Mahogany. First and last. She's Mahogany. Period."

Gina pursed her lips like she wanted to spit, to dismiss Mahogany out of hand, but you didn't forget Mahogany that easily. No one did. That was her power. Another one of them.

I didn't know what to say to get us past it, so I changed the subject. "Where'd they go? Did you see anything?"

Gina pushed up off the wall, stood up to meet me. She had a challenge in her eyes, still, and I knew I'd made the wrong move.

"You should see her guy," I said. "Torrance. He's muscle from ear to ear."

That got a slight smile out of her, so I pressed on. I took her hand in mine. "Listen, we're on this thing together. She's nothing to me, a business connection. She's still hunting Mody."

"Mody?" she said. "M&Ms? I thought you brought him back to SF. You told that Koloa guy he's in jail."

I glanced at the elevators, wanting to know whether we had a floor to go stake out, if she knew where the suits had gone. But Gina didn't move. I showed her my hands. The crescents had faded from my wrist.

"Mody got out. He slipped the police. Likely he's here making a play for the sneakers himself."

"He's—" She stopped. "Of *course* he is. How can we find him?"

"We don't. We find the sneakers and avoid him. Mody's small potatoes compared to these kicks. Didn't you hear that story? The Jordans, MJ, Donald Trump?"

She smiled. Nodded. "I don't know," she said. "Something about how she looked at you. It pisses me off."

"Yeah," I said. "She does that. She looks at me like I'm a slab of meat."

"Like you're just a breathing apparatus for your cock." She smiled and grabbed a handful, right there by the elevators. I'm not going to say it didn't turn me on. "*My* cock," she said, squeezing. She brought her face right up to mine. "Don't you forget that, okay?"

"Yes, ma'am." I knew what to answer in that situation. No question.

She kissed me fast on the lips and then let go after a final squeeze. "Twenty-eight and thirty-three," she said. "They got into an elevator that stopped on those two floors. Then it came down empty. Without them."

"Those are Larry Bird and Wayne Embry's numbers."

"Larry Bird and who?"

"Wayne Embry. He's an old Celtic. I'm not even sure how I knew that. Sometimes I find strange things kicking around in the recessed areas of my drug-addled brain."

"Well, pick one," she said. "You watch one floor. I'll watch the other. We try to find what room they're in."

"Yeah. Maybe they'll even make it easy on us and post guards outside the door."

She smiled. "Unlikely."

I looked up at the bank of lights above the elevators, thinking about the possible floors: twenty-eight and thirty-three. Starting at the top made sense. Anyone thinking about dealing for million-dollar sneakers would stay high up, get the nicest room.

"I'll take thirty-three, Larry Bird, and we go from there."

"Twenty-eight then," she said.

We stepped toward the elevators for the higher floors, waited for one to open, and then stepped inside. Then we pressed buttons, the doors closed, and the elevator launched into express. We went straight up, fast, and I had to swallow hard to un-pop my ears.

49

Larry Bird

I said goodbye to Gina on twenty-eight, kissed her and wished her luck, told her to be careful and not to let any thick-necked suits see her before she saw them. Then she was gone, but only a phone call or a text message away.

On thirty-three, the doors opened, and I gave a quick look to be sure the elevator bay was clear of suits. It was, so I stepped out. Next, I moved to the hall, craned my neck to check up and down for any suits guarding a door—that would have been too easy, both for them and for me. I didn't see anything.

I texted down to Gina: *33 empty. Waiting.*

The hallway wasn't long. Leave it to Times Square real estate: even a fancy hotel like this didn't sprawl. All its rooms came on a single line; no wrapping corridors, no turns, nothing extra. Two choices: left or right.

I stood in the middle, wondering what to do, or if I should do anything.

A text came through from Gina: *Same here.*

While I waited, I pulled up Mody's contact info that I'd snatched on the plane to SFO. Maybe it was time to check in with the man. Not to let on what I knew, but to see if he was around or had anything to offer. I pressed the call button and listened.

A few seconds passed. Then it started to ring in my ear. I listened, counted two rings. Then I realized I could hear something faint coming from down the hall, a soft, distinct sound that a part of my brain recognized right away. I put the phone away from my ear and listened: a hard guitar chord and a keyboard. Familiar. Then the sounds were gone.

I listened to my phone: Mody's voicemail, telling me to leave a message.

"No fucking way," I whispered it carefully, not wanting to be heard. But I could swear I recognized the chords. "No way."

I hung up and called Mody's number again, but also started padding softly down the hall, in the direction I thought I'd heard the music. In a few moments, my phone showed the connection going through; the timer started counting. Faint music started a few doors down: keyboards. Like a countdown and... drums. I recognized exactly what I was hearing: the intro music from the 1990s-era Chicago Bulls.

Then it was gone.

"From North Carolina," I whispered, "at guard, six-six..."

That was enough.

I didn't know what was more remarkable or ridiculous, Mody being here, or his having the Bulls intro as his ringtone. This fucking guy. I took a few more steps down the hall. Behind one of the doors, I heard talking in a room. The others around me were quiet.

I had found our man. Room 3315. I texted Gina: *Got him. Guess who?*

Then I leaned toward the door, put my ear up to the wood.

No sound. If the room had three big suits and Mody inside, I would hear *some*thing. Maybe I'd been wrong.

Then a voice came: muffled, but distinctly from inside the room. A deep voice, definitely a man's. Then another.

I couldn't recognize either voice or what was said, but I knew someone was in there. I tried calling him again, listening for a ring inside the room, but also wondering this time if he'd answer.

Nothing happened. Straight to voicemail.

I texted: *It's Jack. Emergency. Need to talk. Danger.*

Maybe some of the news about La Familia would have spooked him by now. If he had any sense, that is. But Mody was a man on a mission: him against all logic, against the world. I knew what he was willing to risk, and it was all of it. Everything.

I texted again: *911.*

Why not?

Then I heard another voice from inside the room. Mody knew what the shoes were worth; he could make a deal in the seven figures, it would all be worth it for him. But he'd also be wide open to a lot of danger. Maybe he'd know enough to be scared.

I watched my phone's screen. No response.

Then a text from Gina: *Who? What should I do?*

From inside the room, I heard footsteps coming towards the door. I ducked back down the hall, away from the elevators and toward the emergency exit stairs. I didn't dare open the door, instead tried to flatten myself against it, to disappear into the doorframe. One-handed, I texted Gina to stay put.

The door to 3315 opened. Out stepped three men, wearing

suits. *My* three men. All of them empty handed. One guard took just a quick look down the hall, and didn't see me. Maybe they weren't even looking. Their business was done. I watched them walk toward the elevators, not speaking, but with a peppier step than they had before. These were guys who'd just gotten paid.

My phone vibrated, and I smothered it against my body. I almost didn't want to look, didn't want to check the hallway to see if any of the three looked back. When I did, they hadn't.

I checked my phone. It was Gina. *On my way up.*

Not the first time a woman had missed the concept of a text from me.

Go to thirty-five, I texted. The last thing I wanted was Gina stepping out of an elevator into our suits. I listened carefully, waited. She didn't text.

Down the hall, I heard the ring of an elevator arriving. I waited what must have been twice the normal time you'd expect it to take for the doors to open and shut. I barely breathed. Finally, I risked a fast peek down the hall. It was empty.

I felt a wash of relief.

Gina texted, *Why?*

I wrote back for her to give me five minutes. Then I went right to the door of 3315. I knocked and waited.

No one spoke inside. I heard no sounds at all.

I knocked again, this time loudly. "It's Jack. Let me in."

Silence from inside. I tried looking in through the fisheye, didn't see anything. Maybe a shadow passed across what I saw. Likely not.

If the room was really empty, if suits had stashed the shoes inside, maybe I could get at them. I tried rattling the door handle, shaking the door. Nothing. I looked through my wallet for a card I didn't need and found an old hotel key from the Sir Francis Drake, shoved this in between the door and its frame where the lock should be. I wiggled it around, ran it up and down.

Nothing.

Pressed my ear against the door. No sounds.

I knocked again on the door. "Hello?"

Waited.

The Jordans were in there, I knew it.

Then I heard a soft voice from inside say, "What is it?"

"Mody?" It was definitely him. "Open this door."

"What do you want?"

"I got to talk to you about the shoes. We have serious buyers. And I know what they're worth."

No response. I listened to my own breathing, hoping Gina wouldn't show up right away. I wanted to try working Mody on my own.

"Just let me in," I said. "This is something good for us both."

"You still work for Leonardi?"

"No way, man. I'm on my own and I'm not taking you back. Just here to see the kicks."

He laughed. The door opened, but the metal latch was still on the catch. I could see one of his eyes and part of his mouth. "What is it?" he asked, "What you got?"

"David Stern," I said. "I can get you an audience with the Angel of Stern. We'll pitch the shoes to him, to keep the NBA's name clean. It's a slam dunk." I chuckled.

"So you heard the whole story."

I rapped on the door. "Come on man, let me in there. We'll do this."

"What'd you get?"

"Donald Trump, Phil Knight, David Stern, Jordan's retirement. All that business. I believe you've got the real thing."

"No, I don't," he said. "They're fakes."

The door slammed. I looked up and saw Gina in the hall. "What the hell was that?" she asked.

"Mody's inside. He says the shoes are fake."

"*What?*"

50

Jesus Shuttlesworth

Five minutes later, after a long string of colorful four-letter words out of Gina, extended pounding on the door by us both, a series of threats to Mody's manhood—again courtesy of Gina—he opened up.

We walked into a newly cleaned hotel room with a king-sized bed, a big flat-screen television, a desk and chair, and a loveseat with a coffee table. By New York standards, the room was plush. I would almost say it was large.

In the middle of the desk was a box. The box. But not *the* box. Its gold wasn't right. It was just cardboard, not metal, and nothing that resembled gold leaf. I went right to it and looked inside, where I found a pair of Jordan Elevens with gold patent leather on them. But these weren't *the* shoes. The first thing I noticed was the lack of jewels.

"The fuck are these?" I asked, holding one up.

"Ray Allens," Mody said. "A player exclusive Nike made when he won his second ring. They're hard to track down, for sure, maybe even worth a grand. But still. These are useless."

"Basically bullshit," Gina said, "just to clarify."

"Yeah. These are worth nothing compared to all I've been

through." He sat down heavily on the bed.

I put the shoe back in the box and unwrapped both of them completely. They were Jordan Elevens, sure. High top with gold leather around the bottom where the patent leather should be. But it wasn't the Saudi Set. Not the Maltese I had seen on Kauai.

On the tongue, "Ray" was written in script. The number on the back was 34—his number with the Heat.

"These are bunk, but they feel valuable. They're light." I bounced the box in my hand.

Mody said, "Ray is an all-time great, but he never should've left the Celtics for the Heat."

"Fuck the Heat."

Mody and I shared a look, something confirming that we both agreed on one of the few basic tenets of our sport. Whatever LeBron had done in going to Miami was wrong. Ray Allen joining him just made it worse.

Mody laughed. "New Big Three, right? How many Big Threes are we going to have?"

"I grew up with the Celtics," I said. "There's only one Big Three and it has Kevin McHale and Robert Parish."

Mody nodded. "Even as far to the west as anyone could be, I respected that team. But I was a Lakers man."

"At least we're getting somewhere."

I wanted to ask him how he got away from the police in San Francisco, but didn't get to before Gina spoke up.

"What the fuck? Enough of the reminiscing. MJ won more titles than Magic or Bird." She snapped her fingers. "So less talk about these shoes and more about how we get back the real ones. Who fucked you, Meyer?"

"The Koloas," I said. "Nobody else, right?"

Mody made a face like he wasn't sure, so I jumped in to let him know we had tailed the suits all the way from the Koloas' hotel. "No way they made a switch. It was those brotherly fucks. They sold you the wrong kicks."

"But how did they know?"

I said, "You called them, right? What'd you say? That the Maltese were fakes and to get whatever they could for them?"

"No." He shook his head. "I didn't do that. I gave them a buyer, said I had set it up. I paid them two-hundred large for these!" He waved at the box of Ray Allens.

"Where'd you get two hundred grand?" I asked, then realized I knew the answer.

Gina said, "And what did you pay those suits to be your bag men?"

Mody shook his head again. All of this was getting billed right back to the SF mob, and their costs were adding up. So was the size of the hole Mody was digging for himself.

I stepped closer to him. "Just to clarify, you were trying to undercut the Koloas on the kicks, anyway. So you fucked them first. They just gave you back the same."

I saw the look in Gina's eye change from uncertainty to guilt. She knew what I had done: that we had just given Leno some clue of what the Maltese were really worth. So it was on us now, too.

How they got the Ray Allens or even knew about them, who could say? Info from some rare sneakerhead knowledge base. More I didn't know.

"So we fucked up," Gina said. She took one of the Ray Allens out of the box and threw it at the bed. It bounced off the pillows and lay on the bed, still looking good. "Now let's go get the real thing back."

Mody stood up. "Those belong to me." I laughed, but he was serious, shot me a look like stone. "Where are they staying?"

I said, "The Hotel @ Times Square. With a leaf on top of the 'at' symbol to make it look like an apple."

Gina said, "It's cute."

He grabbed his jacket off the desk chair. It looked like he'd bought it here in New York. It was a thick leather trench coat. Apparently he was sparing no expense.

"Nice coat," I said.

Mody didn't answer. He just said, "Let's go do this. Let's go get my shoes."

51

Toe to Toe

Gina rode down to the lobby first in an elevator to check whether Mahogany and Torrance were around. When she texted up the okay, I rode down with Mody. Gina met us as the doors opened, and we smuggled Mody out through the short side of the Marriott's lobby, into the insanity of Times Square on a Friday evening.

You could call this tourist central: crowds thick enough to lose anybody shorter than a seven-footer; even at six-foot-four, I could go unnoticed. In between TKTS hawkers, bright lights, and giant-screen advertisements, you could lose just about anything. Or anyone.

Gina led us straight through the mayhem, brought us right back to the Hotel @ Times Square. By the time we crossed Sixth Avenue, the crowds had thinned to normal levels. This time the front desk clerk didn't try to stop us from going right to the penthouse elevator and all the way up to the suites.

On the top floor, Gina pointed him to *C*, and Mody went right over, started pounding on the door.

"Open up, you fucks!"

Gina turned to me and leaned closer. "Is he really under

control?" she asked. "Or do we care?"

I shrugged. "Not at this point. No."

We both watched to see what would happen. For all we knew, the Koloas would be out on the town celebrating with Mody's money or off trying to sell the real Jordans to David Stern, Mecca and Hassan, whoever.

Instead, Leno opened the door like we were all pals. This just kept getting weirder.

"Hello!" He greeted Mody warmly, with a hand-clap and a one-armed bro hug. He led us inside the suite, which looked considerably smaller and shabbier than Mody's at the Marriott, with wallpaper straight out of the Best Western catalog. Even if this was a penthouse, it was cut-rate, at best.

Gina was never one to pull a punch. "This place is worse than a Super 8," she said. "Why didn't you get a real hotel?"

The toilet flushed, and Eddie walked out of the bathroom from our side, surrounded by a cloud of stank. We had to move to get out of his way. Behind us, the door to the outside hall had just closed, and this put Gina and myself between the closet, Mody and Eddie, boxed in.

She said, "Smells like an ass bomb in here. Plus feet."

Eddie laughed. "It's gonna get a whole lot worse."

I could hear the bathroom fan, which meant the bathroom door was open, which meant we were all in a lot of trouble. "How about we all step out into the hallway?" I said, but the door wouldn't open without everyone moving further into the room.

Mody turned that idea down cold. "Fuck that," he said. "I want the shoes. Now." He was ready to move in on Leno, but

Eddie put a hand on his shoulder to hold him back. That gave Gina and me just a bit of the space we needed.

Leno laughed. "You said to sell 'em to those dudes. So we did. Now what? Go ask *them* for the kicks."

"You know exactly what I'm talking about, you little prick?"

"Do I?"

Eddie pulled Mody back away from Leno and pushed him into the open closet. He bounced off the tiny safe, knocked down some hangers, and fell onto the luggage rack.

"Maybe you better tamp it down, little buddy. Think about what's going on." Eddie was taller than Mody by a foot, at least.

The rack and some hangers fell around Mody as he struggled to get up.

The smell from the bathroom reached us, and Gina groaned, pulled her shirt up to cover her mouth and nose. "Can somebody *please* close that door?"

Leno stepped forward next to his brother. Now they both looked down on Mody like they owned him. So much for the old-friends treatment. "You think I didn't know that buyer worked for you? How much you spend on his time today? And waste on his weak-ass muscle?"

"Weak," Eddie said.

Somehow Mody had gone from the man I knew in Hawaii to someone who spared no expense. Those suits would cost at least ten grand in San Francisco dollars, even more with a New York markup. So Mody had pulled out all the stops, a fact that told me the sneakers were real, within our reach, and that he already had a buyer—a *big* one. He managed to stand up by bracing his hands against the closet's sides.

I wanted to get out of the entryway and scan for the gold-leafed box in the suite, but Eddie stood in my way, staring down Mody like he wanted to throw him *through* the closet.

Leno said, "I mean, two hundred grand? You think we don't know shit about these kicks now? Even your boy Jack Palms knows about the whole conspiracy theory, David Stern, Jordan's gambling. But I'll take your money. *And* the shoes."

Eddie laughed, pushed Mody back into the closet like it was an afterthought. "What you gonna do?"

"So Mody fucked up," Gina said. "Give us all a break and close the bathroom door. Then let's go sell some fucking sneakers."

"Sell the Ray Allens," Leno said. "Go ahead." He laughed. "*If* we have the Maltese, we sure ain't giving them to you."

But Eddie had finally heard Gina and caught some level of pity or embarrassment; he turned away to close the bathroom door. It wouldn't make a difference in the room's air supply, but it provided my opening.

I moved through Leno and into the larger part of the room. "Where are the kicks?"

I saw the night table, two beds, some crappy art on the walls, and a big TV standing on a long armoire that ran along one full side of the room. Beyond the beds was a lounge chair with an ottoman. A suitcase lay open on it, but there was no sneaker box in it, nothing worth noting. The bed closest to me had an open suitcase on it, too. Again, no sneakers.

The first hiding places that came to mind were under the beds and the drawers of the armoire. Mody had ruled out the closet, the safe inside it was way too small, and the bathroom would be an insult to Mike, all of basketball history, and sneakerheads everywhere.

I turned back to Leno. "Where are they?"

He started toward me, and I dropped into a comfortable stance, bending my knees so I was ready to move with his attack, fend him off, or counter-punch as needed. Behind him, I knew I had only a moment or two before Eddie did his worst to Mody and maybe Gina.

Leno came at me in a variety of bull charge that he must've learned from his older brothers. It was straight Koloa Playbook and easily redirected, especially for an attacker who didn't pack the physical mass of his brothers. I pivoted on my front foot with my back to the bed, letting his kinetic energy sweep through the area I had just occupied. I kicked the side of his closest leg, knocking him off balance, and pulled his shoulders in the opposite direction. He flopped beside me, right in between the beds and onto the floor by the night table. He would be back up in a few moments, but that gave me the time I needed to focus on his big brother.

Mody was standing his ground in front of the closet. Like a good soldier, Gina had already moved away from the door, following Leno's path into the room. Now she stood by the far bed and looked to be sizing up Leno for an attack of her own.

"Kick his ass," I told her.

Then I saw Eddie in the hall. He was squared up with Mody, ready to drop the little man, and that was his mistake. He should've been focusing on me, watching what I did to his brother.

For once in his life, Mody ducked, avoided taking a punch,

and Eddie swung a big right hand through the air. I stepped around with my right foot, pivoting again on my left, and brought all the momentum from my hips up into a right hook to Eddie's ribs. He puffed out from the blow to his lung, and staggered left, caught off balance by his own momentum and my added force. The hallway wall caught him. He bumped against it and fell back toward me.

"Help Gina," I said fast, and Mody moved.

In the tight space, it wasn't a time to pull punches, so I did what I had to. I hit Eddie in the groin with a right uppercut from my knees that doubled him in a hurry.

Getting punched in the nuts is strange: it actually doesn't hurt for a second or three, but the fear, the shock of seeing it happen, *that* paralyzes a man and sends him into the fetal position ahead of time. Without this response, he could still fight for the two to four seconds before his insides turn to molten jelly.

I didn't wait; I hit Eddie with a short left hook to one side of his head, and another quick right to the other. He was reeling, but not out or down, so I pushed him back toward the bathroom. He hit the door, I chopped the handle to open it, and he tumbled inward, onto the tiles. I saw him falling toward the commode, knew if I was lucky, he'd hit his head on it and really get hurt.

I shut the door fast, held the handle in place to keep him in.

Then next sound I heard was the groan of that lava effect taking over everything in his body below his chest. So much for him getting knocked out on the porcelain throne. I had a minute. Maybe two.

Back in the room, I heard the crash of the night table's lamp—Gina wasting no expense, I hoped.

She and Mody brought Leno around the corner. Mody had him in a headlock, and Gina had one of his arms twisted behind his back.

"Where are the shoes?" I said. "Give 'em up and we're out of your hair."

"Your short hairs," Gina said, giving Leno an extra twist of his arm.

Inside the bathroom, Eddie yelled. He kicked the door, hitting it low. He would still be on his back. Maybe not for long. Another kick, and this one shook the whole doorframe. I didn't know if the hotel materials would take another once he was back to full strength.

"Hurry up."

Mody said, "Where are the shoes?" He pulled Leno's head up and back, cranking it in his headlock.

Leno, give him credit, held in there. "Let's make a deal," he said.

"Gina?"

She twisted his arm again, this time for longer, harder. He squeezed his eyes shut, but didn't say anything. She said, "I can break this shoulder, you know."

Eddie said, "You hurt him, I'll kill you all." He was up now, working the handle from the other side. I looked for something I could use to jam in the way and saw nothing.

Again, Mody said, "Where are they?"

"In here," Eddie said through the door. "Come and get them."

Through his pain, Leno laughed as best he could.

"Fuckers," Gina said.

I said, "No way. Look under the beds."

Gina let go of Leno and went to search the room. He shook his arm out and tried to stand up straight, but Mody held him in place, twisted the headlock harder.

Gina said, "Nothing under the first bed." Then, in a moment, "Nothing under either one."

"Try the drawers." I knew we were running out of options, and Eddie's torque on the door handle was getting stronger. It was all I could do to hold it still with both hands.

From inside, he said, "I told you they in here. Come in and get 'em."

Mody shook his head. I didn't believe the big man, either. But neither could I hold the door shut much longer. I heard Gina sliding the drawers of the armoire open and shut, open and shut. I knew exactly where this was heading.

"Move." I motioned to Mody with my head, and he pulled Leno toward the beds.

Eddie worked the handle. I let it go and stepped away. When he opened the door, I stood right in front of him, ready to go toe to toe with a gorilla.

"Try me," I said. "What you want to do?"

52

Dance

Eddie stood in the doorway, hands by his sides. He looked exactly as pissed off as you could expect a man to be after getting punched dirty. "Okay, Palms," he said. "I'm ready this time."

"That's what you said last time."

I threw a fake toward his head, stepping at him, then came in under his raised arm and hit him sharp with a right hook again in the side, just over his hip bone. He huffed. So far I'd hit him in his ribs, his head, now it was time to go for the soft places.

He tried to grab me by the shoulders, but a left hook—the perfect punch in close range—right into the center of his stomach stopped him for a moment. I could've followed right then with another nut punch, but didn't, wouldn't do that twice.

He took a step back towards the toilet, maybe giving himself more room to operate with his long arms, but in truth he was slow. Too slow, and I was in no mood to mess around with this. I kicked him hard on the inside of his front knee. When the knee buckled, he put a hand down on the sink counter to catch himself. From there, he had no move to avoid the combination I'd been setting him up for. Plus, his head was lower now, perfectly slotted for the left hook, right uppercut one-two that I brought. The key to throwing a good hook in tight quarters, any hook, is to use your hips, all of them, and let your front leg pivot with the left arm and elbow, the whole punch coming in parallel to the ground. That stunned him.

The uppercut is a good punch to keep in tight as well; this punch you throw straight up from the hip, loading it with just the slightest, quick-crouch, and coming up from there. I made a sound unconsciously, as I brought the fist up under his chin. I heard my sound, a breath releasing with a little bit of a tone thrown into it, something I couldn't have planned or desired, and then the clap of his jaw slapping closed as his teeth clanked together.

His head barely went up, but his legs went out. I stepped back, saw him sit down onto the toilet—seat closed—and he was done.

Sure, I could've lined him up for more damage and punishment, but he didn't need any more.

Still, I asked. "You want more?"

He didn't move or answer. Likely he hadn't even heard me yet.

"He's good," Leno said, behind me.

Mody had him up against the wall beside the closet, holding a forearm at his throat.

Gina stood next to them. "Damn, Jack. Show me that later?"

"You know it." I winked at her, channeling my best acting to do it without humor.

"You Koloas are hell as a bunch," I said, "but separately, not much in a fight."

Leno told me to get fucked. I raised my eyebrows at Gina, and she smiled.

"Just tell us where to find the shoes."

"He was right," Leno said, gesturing a hand to the bathroom. "They're in the shower."

"Fuck," Gina said.

I turned back to Eddie. His eyes had come into focus, but he wasn't up off the can. "You good?" I asked. "Enough dancing?"

He gave me a weak thumbs up. I guess he'd have nodded or said something but his jaw and neck weren't up to it.

"Good. In all, you guys take home the two hundred grand back to the islands. That should erase Mody's debt and then some."

"No, almost," Leno said behind me.

"Damn." I turned back to Mody. "How much you into them for?"

Before he could answer, I turned away. "Skip it. You'll handle that later."

I walked into the bathroom, watching Eddie for any sudden moves, and threw back the shower curtain. Sure enough, there was the gold-leafed case in the bottom of the tub.

"Good Jesus." The gold's shine in the bathroom lights struck my eyes.

"Really?" Mody was at my side in a hurry, pushing past me. He got to his knees by the tub, pulled the box to him, and threw open the lid. There, under the black velvet cloth, were the Maltese Jordans, jewel-encrusted and everything.

The *real* Maltese Jordans.

Mody said something that sounded like, "Mama." It might have actually been "Mama." He had been through enough for these kicks at this point. That much was true.

I let out a deep breath. "There they are," I said.

Eddie finally spoke. "They is," he said.

I stepped away from his reach to be sure, but he didn't make a move.

"There it is," I said. "We got 'em. The legend, the myth, the kicks. The real fucking deal."

Mody stood up, holding the open case to his face like he wanted to kiss the sneakers inside. I had to reach in over his shoulder, couldn't help it, and touched the leather of the right one. I felt its supple softness, the unnatural hardness of the gold leaf on top of whatever Tinker put under it, and rubbed my finger over the bumps that were jewels. I touched what looked like a diamond and a ruby.

"Goddamn." I forgot myself for a moment, leaving myself open to any attack from the big Koloa; I just stood there, touching what we'd come so far to get.

And then I realized I was one of three in a small New York City bathroom and that we could all do better. I stepped back. "Guess it's time we officially take these off of your hands."

Gina was right by Mody's side, getting her own look. "This is them? The real ones?"

Mody said softly, "Michael Jordan wore these shoes in the Saudi King's private game. These are them."

"Shit," Leno said, "I'm gonna miss 'em."

I knew exactly what he meant, would feel the same way myself once we sold them, but these weren't the kind of thing any of us should keep. These had a place somewhere else.

"Guess it's time to call David Stern," I said.

Gina laughed. "Can't we just have those guys at the hotel sell them? Those crazy sne'ads in the lobby?"

"Maybe," I said. "Unless you have a buyer?" I waited to hear how Mody would answer, maintaining a close watch on both Koloas as I stepped back into the hall by the suite's main door. Neither brother looked to make any move; the vibe was friendly again, like a single schoolyard gang that had just gone a long way on a very exciting trip.

Mody said, "I have a buyer. The best buyer in the world."

53

Plax

We took the kicks back to the Marriott, hiding them in a suitcase—one of the Koloas'—so nobody in the lobby would get wind of what we had. We smuggled Mody through the lobby again. I half-expected to see Mahogany there, waiting, but she was nowhere to be found. Maybe she was chewing on Torrance or off chasing another lead on Mody somewhere else.

For my part, I was past the point where I'd have handed him over, if that had even been an option. We were taking the Jordans to the end of the line, no matter what that meant. And honestly, I wanted another chance to hold them, to maybe even try them on.

Crazy, I know.

For all their troubles, Mody wrote the Koloas another check to take back to Kauai. I didn't see the figure on it, but whatever his offer, that plus what he paid for the Ray Allens got Leno to smile for the first time I'd seen. Neither brother gave us a hard time about walking out with the Jordans after that. I wanted to ask Mody where he got all this money from, or if he was just bouncing checks his ass couldn't cash, but I figured it was something about New York City, the Con and the chance to really cash in on the sneakers that had him riding high and spending widely. Maybe I didn't care.

Back up on thirty-three, Mody threw the suitcase onto the bed and unzipped it. He lifted the box to his lips and kissed it, gave it a big old smack.

"There you are, my babies. Back with Papa now."

Gina shot me a look with a raised eyebrow, but I held out a calming hand.

"What's the plan, Mody? You selling these at the Con, or you got something happening sooner?"

He turned around to us, holding a gun. I should've seen it coming, known he wouldn't be willing to part with these so easily or cut us in on the deal, not when he'd come so far. Or I should've been watching him closer. Just another part of the whole job where I still operated like an amateur—I made a mental note to think back on it later and be better next time.

The gun was small, probably a Glock, and it had a silencer screwed onto its barrel. He wasn't messing around with New York City cops or loud noises.

I raised my hands. "Really? Do you know how much trouble you can get into for carrying a gun in this city?"

He gave me a sourpuss look, mostly in his lips. "Think I care?"

"Guess not. But don't forget what happened to Plaxico."

If we had been in the Koloas' penthouse, I could have reached out and grabbed the gun, beaten him with it, and walked out with the shoes. But here at the Marriott there was enough room for him to put himself four or five paces from either of us. He backed away toward the windows, holding the shoes, and had enough space to get off a shot before we could reach him.

Gina sucked her teeth. "Want me to take that from him, Jack?"

"Sure." I gestured for her to go ahead, but before she could move Mody turned the gun on her and put a bullet right into the hotel wall above her shoulder.

"Don't," he said. "I'm fucking serious."

She stepped back fast. "Oh, he's *fucking serious.*"

The sound of the shot wouldn't do much to alert hotel security, but I figured we had some small chance that the bullet would travel through the wall into his bathroom, and through that, out into the hallway, but I wasn't holding my breath.

"Where did you get that?" I asked.

"Stakes are high here, Jack. This is everything."

I could see down the barrel of the Glock. It wasn't a sight I had gotten used to or liked.

"Get 'em up. Show me your hands."

I did. Gina did, too.

The way he was smiling had me nervous. I wondered for a moment whether he hadn't gotten involved with the Koloas' meth along the way. If I was ever going to have my answer about his relative level of crazy, I should have had it by then. But I still didn't.

"Who's your buyer?" I was stalling, sure, but also curious.

"The man himself. The Donald. The Hair."

"The Combover?"

Gina said, "You can't be serious!"

His smile somehow got wider. "I'm going to call him now. Then go and meet the man for the exchange."

"He really wants to buy the shoes after all this time? The ones he bet Jordan into needing in the first place?"

"Kind of poetic, isn't it? You have to appreciate that."

"It's literary and all. I believe Hammett would approve."

He laughed. If I knew he liked anything, it was the shoes and a touch of literature in his references. And Hammett or especially Chandler would have liked Trump's entry. Trump was big money, the same power that always pulled the strings behind everything.

The old masters would have thrown in some cops investigating, but on Kauai and now here in New York, there were none to be found. Gone were the days of pressed suits and ties, heroes knowing their local cops and sparring with them verbally over what was right.

Gina said, "How did you get in touch with Trump?"

"Turns out he felt bad about the bet all this time. He contacted *me* once I floated the shoes on the internet. Turns out he's been looking for them all along. That's what started me out of SF with those fucking accountants' money. I had to have the big cheddar to pay off the Koloas and pave the way. But I knew DJT was holding a big purse at the end of the rainbow, so it was always worth it. Worth all of it."

Gina said, "You're fired," making the signature Trump hand gesture.

"Jordan never forgave Trump for that day, the bet, what it made him do. That was the moment he really could have lost it all, the things he cared about most: basketball, his career, his legacy. And you know what? Jordan's not a man to piss off. Even for a guy like Trump, that shit follows you."

I said, "Everybody loves Jordan."

Gina said, "Everybody *hates* Trump."

"So this is the only way Trump thinks he can make it up: get the shoes and give them back to Mike. Take them completely out of circulation and make sure they can never come to light. Kill any chance of that conspiracy ever getting confirmed."

"Shame," I said. "Once Jordan gets them, they'll be just another pair. Those are some really fresh kicks. What if?"

Mody was already shaking his head. "No. Don't even say it." He aimed the gun at me more seriously.

"No, really. What if I just wore them, used them as actual shoes? Come on. They look like they're close to my size." I kept my hands in front of me as I crouched down, started unstrapping and untying my Air Force Ones.

"Get up! You're not going to do this. They're worth far too much."

"How much?" I looked up at him, my hands on my laces.

"Ten," he said. "*Ten million.* Trump'll pay that much to get them back. Would you really wear that much money on your feet? Just let it go by the boards?"

"You said yourself if there was one thing you'd do anything for, that it was *these* shoes. That meant just having them, right? Stowing away that piece of history? Keeping it safe so you were the only one who could see it."

"Yes. No. I mean no." He put his hands out like he was pleading. "It's ten million fucking dollars, Jack. That's everything I could ever want. *Everything.*"

Gina said, "Take the money. Seriously. Just give me like *one* million. Two, actually. *Two.*"

"What's Jordan going to do with them? He'll just want to forget. And you really want to give Donald Trump one less enemy? Don't you think he deserves every single one he's got? Especially the famous ones?"

"Doesn't matter. This way MJ gets them back, maybe he looks me up one day, wants to repay me. Maybe we meet." He shrugged. "Stranger things have happened."

I thought about all I'd been through for a pair of sneakers, the distance from Kauai to San Francisco to New York City, and I couldn't disagree. "He's right," I told Gina.

"So we're not getting a cut?"

"You get to live," Mody said.

"Even after all that? Come on. Just give us a fraction. You're not really going to kill us."

"No? Maybe I'm not. But maybe I am." He nodded toward the door. "Why don't you two just leave. Get out. Don't come back."

I tied my laces back up and re-strapped the shoes. I thought about launching myself from the low position toward Mody's legs, but instead just stood up. "Come on, man. You think we won't be watching every step you take? Think we won't be trailing you right to the Donald and then finding a way to get the shoes back? Or the money?"

He looked at the door, looked back at us. Gears were whirring in his head. He could tell there wasn't a good option that let him do what he wanted to do to us.

"Tie us up?" I said, guessing where he'd go for a next move. "Come on. Like that one hasn't been done before? *Please.*"

I was painting him into a corner that left just one choice, and

I was betting he wouldn't be willing to take it.

"You're so smart then, what should I do?"

"We're partners, man. No way to shake us now. We all go see the Donald. You give us a cut. We've earned that."

Gina had her hands on her hips. "Damn right we have!"

"You really want to see the Don?" Mody asked. "Follow this thing all the way through?

I held my hands by my sides. "Don't fuck with us, man. You wouldn't be here without us."

"Fine," he said, finally, lowering the gun. "I'm calling him right now."

Part IV

The Don(ald)

I thought Jordans and a gold chain was living it up.

54

The Call

Mody stepped to the desk and opened his laptop, still holding his gun. I could see him scrolling through emails, looking for the right one. When he found it, he stood up, pulled his phone out of his back pocket. He typed in the numbers and held the phone to his ear.

"It's ringing."

Gina whispered, "He's actually calling the Donald."

"Still ringing."

"We talking cell phone or a landline?" I asked. "Do you actually have the Donald's cell?"

Gina said, "You're fired. Text him that he's fired."

Mody said, "Hello," into the phone. He paused. "I—" he said. "Yes. This is Meyer Mody calling." Then he held the phone away from his ear, mouthed to us, "They're getting him."

I said, "Never answer your own phone. That's a rule for high rollers."

Gina smiled. "*Never.*"

I considered rushing Mody to take the gun or making a grab for the shoes, but in truth it was more interesting to watch and see how things played out. I cared less about my cut now, more about the shoes and where they ended up. This had stopped being about money a long time ago.

But yeah, I'd take a cool few million.

And I still wanted to see the SneakerCon the next day, too. What better place to start spending it?

"Hello," Mody said, finally. "Yes. Yes, it's nice to finally talk to you, too." His chin wrinkled like mine would have if Donald Trump was actually nice to me. "Thank you, Mr. Trump. Yes. Okay. Yes, sir."

He held the phone away from his ear and smiled, choked back a laugh.

Gina said, "He's fucking with us, right? That's not Trump. He's *never* nice."

I said, "That's just his TV personality. It's a front for a big softie." We both laughed. "Yeah, right."

Gina sang the words, "Douche-bag," like they were two parts of a chorus.

Mody said into the phone, "I can do that. Yes. Yes, a car would be perfect. The Marriott Marquis. Yes. Ten minutes. Great."

He listened for a time, then thanked Trump again and hung up.

Mody looked at us cold. "Trump said I have to come alone."

"Bullshit! There's no way you go see the Donald without us. What else did he say?"

"He's picking me up. I'm going to Trump International. That's the meet. The car's coming now, and he said it's just for me."

"Get the shoes," I told Gina.

She jumped onto the bed and threw herself at the shoebox,

slid across the comforter toward the pillows with it. Mody turned his gun on her, but didn't shoot. I had bet right. By the time he knew what was happening, I was on him, wrestling with him for the gun. I had his arm, used my knee to knock the shit out of his wrist not once, but twice, and he dropped the gun. It fell to the floor, didn't go off, and I picked it up.

I stepped back toward Gina, aimed the gun at Mody.

"Some trip, huh?" I said.

"He's on his way. Trump. He's expecting to pick up me. He *knows* me."

Gina laughed. "Like hell he does."

"So what do we do?" I asked Gina. "Maybe we just leave our boy to see Trump himself empty-handed? Think the Donald would like that?"

She held the shoebox in front of her, sitting with it on her lap. With one fingernail, she scratched at the lid, peeled off a scab of the gold leaf.

"What are you doing?" Mody said.

I was pretty shocked myself.

She held the flake in front of her face, turning it in the light, then opened her mouth and placed it on her tongue.

I felt my eyes grow as she closed her mouth around the gold.

After a moment, she coughed and spit it out into her hand. "I always wanted to try that."

"Doesn't melt."

"No," she said. "Tastes like metal."

"This isn't *Goldmember*," I said. "What did you expect?"

She opened the box and looked inside, sniffed the rare air of His Airness's feet. I wanted to do the same. "How do they smell?"

"Like old."

"Time's ticking," Mody said. "Trump's on the way. Let's ditch the gun and get real about this."

"I'll meet him," I said.

"Like hell." Gina looked at me with her brows knit. She held one of the shoes in her hand, fondling the rubies. "It's all three of us now. We have to do this together."

I laughed, turned to Mody and laughed again. "This idiot just pulled a fucking gun on us!"

They both stopped, staring at me. They'd believed my whole line about us three together. Eaten it right up. They both wanted it that way.

"Really?" I said. "You're serious?"

Gina said, "Like death. We can't cut him out now."

"He just had a gun on us." I showed it to her. "This gun!"

She unfolded her legs and slid off the bed, held out the box to me. "Go ahead, Jack. Touch them. You know you want to."

She was right.

"Shit."

I slid my hand in through the black velvet and pulled out the left shoe. My palm slid along its bottom and my first thought was that it was *big*. Bigger than I expected. With The Man's shoe in my face, I was struck first by the size of it, half again as long as my hand, if not double. The jewels were sparkling, bigger than any I'd ever seen on an engagement ring. Even in LA's wildest times, I had only seen costume jewelry with stones this big. I fingered the settings, enjoying the feel of the tight connections. I noticed creases along the ball of the foot, where the shoe had bent as Mike played. The tongue looked suspiciously absent of any insignia. No Jumpman silhouette or anything. Just white nylon. I ran my fingers over the signature on the toe.

Then I put my nose to the opening of the shoe. I had to. I smelled its smell. His Airness. As close as I was likely to ever get. It smelled like a shoe that has been sitting away in a box for a very long time. Like old air, she was right.

"Smells like the ocean," Gina said.

"Yeah. Maybe." I brought the sneaker up to my cheek, rubbed the gold leather across my skin. Then I put the shoe next to me on the bed and studied it for a few moments. Then I stood back up. "I needed that. Now I'm good for whatever. Anything."

Mody stepped toward us. I let him, dropped the clip out of the Glock and ejected the chambered round. I put them both by the TV and tucked the gun down the back of my pants.

Mody said, "Let me meet with the Donald myself. I'll make the sale. I can nail it."

"Anything except that. Gina's right: we all go for this, whether Trump likes it or not."

55

Jimmy Choo

As we rode the elevator down to the lobby, I had a premonition; the idea struck me that we had rolled these dice one too many times. I had a mind to press the button for two, get off there and take the stairs, something, but I didn't. I just watched things happen in front of me like I was asleep at the wheel.

Maybe I was. It had been a day, and a night and a day, and then some. I was in the moment and—in some sense—just watching things flow. I was ready to take on what happened next.

So I wasn't surprised or upset when the elevator doors opened to the lobby and the first person standing there was Torrance. I stepped out in front of him, Mody and Gina behind me, and said, "Hey man. What's up?"

Torrance looked like he'd just come from the hotel gym; he wore a tight black tank top with thin shoulder straps to show off his muscles, gray shorts, and sneakers. I didn't bother to see what they were. "Welcome to the show," he said, spreading his arms.

Behind him the crowd of Sn'eads had increased by a lot. Now a couple hundred people were milling around in the lobby, some even carrying stacks of sneaker boxes in their arms and comparing their pairs with others'. Maybe they had even started trading and selling.

Torrance pointed his chin over my shoulder. "I see you got something I been looking for."

Mody.

One move would be to let him have the guy, give over M&Ms and say goodbye once and for all. But I couldn't. Not least because he was my in with The Orange One. No, even if walking away with the Jordans myself would be easier, I had to stand up for what was mine, for whoever was now a part of my posse.

Torrance wasn't as big as Eddie Koloa, but he took way better care of himself. Plus, if he worked for Mahogany, he'd be good with his hands. She hadn't gotten this far by fighting the rebellious runners herself.

"Where's your boss?" I asked.

Gina stepped beside me, on my right. Mody stood on my left, a little behind me.

An icy voice said, "I'm right here."

Perfectly on time, as always, Mahogany stepped out of the elevator next to ours. Maybe her man had a mic on, or maybe she'd heard exactly what she needed—her timing would be that good. She stepped smoothly next to Torrance, wearing a different black dress, this one preposterously even tighter-fitting, and a short black jacket that barely came down to her waist.

I said, "Damn, woman. You do know how to make an entrance."

She smiled at me—that super-seductive *fuck me* smile that I knew would make Gina's blood boil.

"Right here and right on time," she said, cool as you please, placing a hand on Torrance's shoulder. "And I see you have something I want."

"But you have something *I* want." Gina stepped in front of me, right up to Mahogany. She gave up three or four inches, even with them both wearing heels, but still looked her right in the eye.

Mahogany lowered her eyes to meet Gina's like she was lowering her whole self to a pedestrian level, as if it took her some real effort to scan down those few inches. "Yes," she said, as if her words came out of a walk-in freezer. "And what, possibly, is that?"

"*That,*" Gina said, pointing behind Mahogany with her left hand.

I didn't expect this, so I looked, saw just the other side of the elevator bay, a triptych of closed doors. Mahogany did the same, and so did Torrance, just for a second. That was all the time Gina needed.

She cold-cocked Mahogany in the jaw, sucker-punched her right there in her Jimmy Choos, and laid the woman out.

I barely saw it, it happened so fast. Torrance missed it too, but managed to catch his woman as she fell.

"Holy shit," Mody said.

Gina had her knuckles to her mouth, then shook out her hand. I could tell it hurt; she'd had no idea how to hit someone like that. But she had. And it *worked*. Mahogany was ready for smelling salts, an icepack, whatever. Torrance held her down by our knees.

"The fuck," he said.

"*Damn.*" I placed a gentle hand on Gina's shoulder, not wanting to surprise her.

People around us started to gather, asking if Mahogany was okay, what happened, what they could do to help. A security guard stepped forward talking into a walkie-talkie, asking for a medic. "Is she all right?" he asked.

I nudged Gina away from the commotion, toward the lobby, as a circle began to close around Torrance and his boss.

"Time to go," I said.

I heard Torrance call to us, but he couldn't leave her or get up to follow.

Mody came right along, carrying the gold sneaker box close to his chest.

While everyone was focused on Mahogany, I took the chance to pull Mody's Glock from my waistband and ditch it in a potted plant. I pushed it into the dirt to the grip as we walked by, left it there for some sneakerhead to take home as a memento.

56

All the Way Up

Five minutes later, the three of us sat in the back of a black town car, driven by one of Trump's flunkies and headed uptown. His man wore a black suit, actually had a black chauffeur's hat on to match it. I guess when you've got money like Trump and a complex about proving it, chauffeur's hats make sense.

The driver kept quiet, didn't mention that there were three of us instead of just one. I held the Maltese Jordans on my lap, feeling the cold metal, breathing the air of their legend, glad to have dropped off the gun. No way was I going down as the guy who took a Glock to Trump's lair, where pat-downs and metal detectors were sure to be a matter of course.

From Times Square, the chauffeur took us west to 8th Avenue and then straight up to Columbus Circle, where we rounded to Central Park West and pulled up in front of Trump International.

Valets opened the rear doors for us. I had been sitting behind the driver, so I got out first, looked around to be sure no one snapped pictures under the bright lights. As far from the paparazzi as I'd been, and for this long, this was not the time or the place I wanted them snapping pics of me again. Not holding an unexplainable, doesn't-exist, golden sneaker box. And the red carpet was right there. Trump left no other way to enter his building.

I swore someone said my name, then another. "Palms," I heard, "Jack Palms."

I clutched the box to my chest. Someone's camera flashed, and a valet rushed to make sure it didn't happen again.

"Right inside, please. Mr. Trump is upstairs waiting."

I had a flash that I should run, take the shoes right to Jordan myself, to make sure they never hit the press, to bring them right to the man, but it was just that: a flash. The kicks were headed home.

Mody stood next to me, waiting for me to make a move.

"You sure you want to do this?" I asked.

"Shit yes," Gina said, behind us, pushing us forward with a hand at the small of each of our backs.

Valets held open glass doors for us to enter a small vestibule off to the side of the main lobby. From there, another man pointed us to a private elevator with polished brass doors. "Please," he said.

As we stepped toward it, Mody said, "Yeah. This is what we do."

"Okay." As I walked to the elevator, the doors slid open. A man inside stood waiting to operate it for us. I got in it, followed by my friends.

There were only two buttons on the elevator's panel: L and T. Did "T" stand for Top? Or Trump? I didn't ask. Instead I swallowed hard, expecting a fast rise to the top.

Above the second story, the elevator's shaft was made of glass.

So, too, was the car. We turned around to watch the city. I could see out over Central Park as we rode upward, higher and higher until I could see more of Manhattan: first the highest buildings of Midtown, the Empire State Building, the beacon of light shooting upwards that was present-day Times Square, and then below that to downtown, as well as all the way up to Harlem in the north.

As the car finally started to slow, I saw the Statue of Liberty herself, the grand old lady who had seen so much and for so long. How things had changed before her eyes.

I looked at Gina beside me. "How's your hand, champ?"

She smiled. "Damn, it hurts, but that felt so fucking *good.*"

I wanted to kiss her, but the elevator slowed down suddenly, and it caught me off guard. My ears popped, and I swallowed, then turned back toward the doors.

If my life had led me to this, if this was the extent of the heights I would attain without fame or acting or my own Hollywood-earned riches, then I could make do with it. I breathed in a deep breath of this rare air, held the gold-leafed box of His Airness's game-worn 1996 Maltese Jordans in my hands, those kicks covered in jewels, and I was at the absolute apex of New York City, about to see Donald J. Trump himself, mayor of the block, the crown prince of capitalism, the Wizard of Oz, the ruler of all.

The elevator doors slid open.

I was ready.

57

Appraisal

"Here we are," the elevator operator said in a quiet voice.

Outside the elevator, I saw a grand reception area: thick rugs, deep, dark wooden furniture, Picassos and Lichtensteins on the walls.

A woman's accented voice announced, "Right this way."

She stepped forward to greet us, a white woman, likely from far parts of the globe, wearing a white robe and stocking feet. She was dressed like a geisha, but tall and blonde, even more beautiful than I'd have imagined.

Gina punched me in the side, a perfect kidney shot. "Watch it, Jack."

"I am."

She hit me again.

The woman led us across the lobby and opened a door that was practically invisible in the wall. The ground felt soft under my feet, like we were walking on a three-inch thick carpet on top of foam.

Gina shoved her way in front and walked through the door first. I followed her into a boardroom that looked just like the one from television, from the pressure-filled meetings at the end of his shows.

I half expected to see three chairs waiting across from us, complete with the old guy and the skinny blonde lady, but instead, there were no chairs at the table at all. Just a long, shiny stretch of dark wood. Beyond that, a window with a view over Central Park, towards the east side.

"We're really here," Gina said.

The geisha woman turned around. "Excuse me?"

"No. Nothing," Gina said.

The door closed behind us, and the woman said, "Please set the box on the table, Mr. Palms."

I stepped up and did as asked. Suddenly things had taken a strange turn, as if the Donald was not about to greet us with generosity, warmth, and offers of the finest scotch.

"Where is he?" I asked.

"Who?" the woman said.

Before I could answer, another door opened and a small man walked in, wearing slacks, a white shirt with suspenders, and glasses. On his head was a jeweler's visor. He crossed to the window-side of the table and stood across from us, regarding us each for a moment.

"Yes," he said. Then he went for the box: he lifted it toward him, then placed it on a thin rubber mat on his side of the table. As he did, he ran his fingers along its edges, as if checking for dents. Another woman, dressed as the first but with black hair, appeared from the back of the room carrying a gooseneck lamp. She plugged into an outlet in the center of the table and set it down in front of the jeweler, next to the shoes. He clicked it on.

Then he lowered the visor with the big magnifier lenses and fitted it over his eyes.

I whispered to Mody, "Are they real?"

"The people?" He shrugged. "I know the Jordans are."

I counted my breaths. We had come a long way.

The little jeweler regarded all of this as if it were a matter of course, as if things like lamps always appeared just where he needed them. Without taking his eyes off the box's lid, he angled the lamp and adjusted its neck to get better light. He bent lower to get an even closer look, running his finger pads across the box's corners.

"Tastes like gold," Gina said.

Her words broke the silence so abruptly and were met with so little that I expected to hear their echoes. Instead, I watched the jeweler lift the lid of the box and reach in to move the black velvet out of his way. He removed the sneakers one by one, set them down neatly side by side. Next, he removed the velvet entirely and spread it out on the table. He rubbed it flat, inspecting the golden insignias of the Jumpman logo, then set it aside. Next he ran his fingers all along the inside of the box, checking it, looking carefully with the lamp, then closed it and slid the box to the side.

He stood up straight, lifted his visor, and regarded us again. With pursed lips, he struck me as doctorly, a man I could trust. Such was the jeweler of Trump. For a moment his mouth opened, and I thought he might say something, but that passed. He closed his mouth again and turned back to the sneakers.

At first he just stared at them for maybe thirty seconds. Several long breaths. I wondered how much of this it would take, but knew we weren't supposed to protest. However long it took this man to render his verdict, Trump would wait, somewhere, and so would I.

When he moved next, it was to lift the left shoe and bring it close to his face. He smelled its interior, just like I had.

"His Airness," I said.

Gina said, "Smells like ocean, right?"

The jeweler inhaled a longer breath than I had, took his time smelling the insole and whatever else happened to wind up inside a sneaker preserved for eighteen years. Then he gave a slight nod, set the sneaker down, and lifted the other one. He lowered his visor, adjusted the magnifier, and studied the tread of the right shoe under the lamp, spending a lot of time around the ball of the foot. Finally, he smelled the rubber.

"Interesting," he said. His accent sounded Eastern European, not New York.

"What?" I couldn't help myself.

"Tread wear indicates a lot of cutting," he said, without glancing up. "Stops and starts. Changes of direction."

I said, "You've seen the man play, right?"

A wry smile let us know this man was not one of the few uninitiated. Everyone knew Michael Jordan's game.

Mody said, "He played hard. Even in a game for the sheik."

"Apparently." The jeweler turned the shoe over and focused on the toe, where the leather and rubber met and the jewels were placed. He made a few changes with his visor, turned down a bigger lens, and bent the lamp to get better light.

He studied each of the jewels, the red ones and the green, and what I guessed had to be diamonds. I wanted to hold the shoes one last time, to have the right in my hand while he studied the left, but I didn't move. I wondered if the Donald was watching us on a screen somewhere. Around the moldings of the far wall were several small globes of dark glass, the kind that contained cameras.

"Is he watching us now?"

No one answered. I looked to see if the women would let on some knowledge, but they had left, slipped out without my notice.

In the distance, I could hear the white noise of fans, the heating system perhaps or just air circulation. Otherwise, quiet. This high above the city, the sounds of the streets couldn't reach us. A plane could fly above the skyline on the other side of the park, and I doubted if we would hear it at all.

"Maybe we should sit?" I asked.

Gina looked around: at the walls, behind us and under the table, made a show of searching for a chair, a couch, anything. There was nothing.

She said, "Apparently, we wait."

The jeweler studied the side of the left shoe, moving his focus around the patent leather gold upper. Finally he put the shoe down on the table, lifted the other. He studied this one more quickly, giving it fewer glances at the stones through his glasses. Then he put them both down together, lined them up so the toes were even, the shoes next to the box, and nodded. When he lifted his visor to regard us, I thought he might smile, but he didn't. Instead he tipped his chin and turned to walk out of the room.

Mody said, "They're real."

"They better be." Gina laughed. "After all this?"

I said, "They are."

At the door, the jeweler stopped, turned back to us for a moment. Now he smiled, even bowed a little. "I believe these to be authentic," he said. "They are the Saudi Arabian Elevens. Mr. Trump will be very pleased."

58

You're Fired

The jeweler left, and the door closed silently on its own.

Then we were alone. I could see us all reflected in the glass of the big window that we stood facing. The three of us and the shoes.

The Maltese Jordans.

The Saudi Set.

The Arabian Elevens.

These were really them.

"You're not full of shit after all," I said to Mody. "How about that."

He chuckled, shaking his head. "You must've had some idea, if you're here."

"Who wouldn't want to follow along for a story like this?"

"And a few million dollars," Gina said.

"I think—" Mody started to say something but he was cut off. The jeweler's door opened again, and this time a valet came through it wheeling a huge leather desk chair. He slid it to the other side of the table.

"What is this?" I said, "For the Wizard of Oz?"

Behind us another door opened and two valets walked in

carrying straight-backed wooden chairs. One held two and the other held just one. They put them down on our side, in front of the table, gestured for us to sit down.

One of them said, "Mr. Trump will be with you shortly." Then they were gone.

We sat down.

Classical music filled the room, alleviating the spookiness of the silence and the hum. I recognized it as something famous that I'd heard before.

When the door opened, I half-expected to hear trumpets blow to announce their king. Instead, it was just the man himself, Mr. Trump, the Donald who walked in. He wore a dark suit, as always, but this time without a tie. His hair was even more garishly combed over his obviously balding head than it seemed on television. It looked like a big red mullet from the side of his hairline had been combed toward his face, but this construction sat there perfectly, as if you might not notice what it was if you looked at him from afar. And yet it was so glaring, so clearly not right that it almost dared you to say something, to call it to his attention.

But none of us did. Of course.

"Gentlemen," he said, as he walked behind the table.

"And lady," Gina said.

Trump laughed, held up his hands. "I apologize for that. Yes, my dear. And how beautiful you are."

He sat down in the leather chair in front of the shoes, pulled them toward him. "These fucking things. Do you believe it?"

I guessed he meant the existence of the legend, asking if we were actual believers, which I knew we all now were, but he

311

could've also been asking about all the trouble or the amount of money he was spending. It wasn't clear. He could've just been asking if we believed that he was here, or that we were.

He tapped the shoes with his fingertips, gazed at them and then at us.

"Just in time for Christmas," he said, "but not really." He shook his head. "Do you know what it's like to have Mike mad at you for this long? Jesus, that man can hold a grudge."

I tried to point out that their little wager had almost cost the greatest basketball player of all time the second half of his career, but Trump raised a hand and I stopped. He had that effect. Call it a power. Mahogany would have been impressed.

"You know the prescription. Take money from some people, beat them honestly, and they hold it against you. It's the story of my life, actually."

Jordan had never seemed the type to me, definitely not a sore loser, and I could see where he'd be pissed about all the trouble, but I kept it to myself.

"Can I say, 'You're fired?'" Gina asked.

Trump nodded. "Of course. People do it all the time."

She said, "You're fired," with a deep voice, making the gun-shaped hand gesture across the table.

He didn't complain.

"Thanks," she said.

"Now then." He reached into his jacket, withdrew a checkbook that he set down on the table. "You'll take a check?" He smiled. "I assume you know I'm good for it."

"Ten million?" Mody said.

Trump waved his hand, as if the figure offended him to be

spoken out loud, as if it was only a small detail.

"Actually, cashier's check only. Or cash."

Trump looked up. "Cash?" He laughed. "Like some kind of silver suitcase full of money in wrapped stacks? No. No, that's not reasonable."

The two of them, Trump and Mody, stared each other down across the table. Each one was calling the other's bluff. I had no doubt that Mody would be the first to fold.

Seconds passed, I breathed in and out, enjoying the fine smell of the room. Gina squeezed my knee under the table. Trump's eyes and hair didn't move.

He waited us out.

Finally, he laughed. "Good for you," he said. The Donald. Trump himself. He slid a separate piece of paper out of his inside pocket and pushed it across the table. "An old joke among businessmen, but one that never fails to amuse me."

I saw the official seal and the gray paper of the check. A cashier's check, stamped and ready. There it was. Mody picked it up.

"Boom," Gina whispered.

Trump stood. I still half-expected him to offer us a drink, share in a fine wine and a toast to the success of our endeavor, but as I looked around for the bar to appear, none did.

He walked around the table to Mody, who got to his feet still staring at the check. Trump pumped his hand once, firmly, to conclude the deal.

Then he moved on to Gina, kissed her on the cheek. We were all standing now and the shoes still on the table.

He turned to me.

"I liked your movie," he said. "A shame about your career, otherwise. Though maybe now you've got some new backers." He thumbed at Mody and Gina. "I'd really love to see a sequel to *Shake 'Em Down*."

We shook hands. He told us to have a good night. Then the jeweler's door opened on its own, and he walked through it.

Suddenly the women were there, ready to escort us out through the other door back into the reception area where I could see the elevator waiting, its open doors beckoning for us to come along.

I let Mody and Gina walk out ahead of me, Mody still holding the check in front of him like an idiot, counting and re-counting the zeroes.

As they walked out, I waited an extra breath, stalling, wanting to remain in that room longer, to stay in the presence of the shoes. I turned to them, still sitting there on the table, lined up next to the box. Trump had barely touched them. To him they were just one more thing. Even less: they were an object of importance for somebody else, a means to handling an unfortunate social interaction, to fixing a bet gone wrong. The money was nothing to him. It was another thing to come in and then out of your life, a figure that changed things temporarily and then didn't.

But the shoes, there they were: the history, the smell, the legend and the connection to greatness; the beauty, the design, the materials, the jewels. I knew I'd never see something else like them, and maybe that was lucky. They had caused one holy fuckload of trouble, but they had also given me something bigger: joy.

I reached out to them, to the shiny leather, the sculpted rubber, the nylon. I touched them one last time, squeezed the back of the left one that would have been closest to His Airness's Achilles. There they were, something to change lives, to make people crazy, to make them do stupid things. Mody would be going back to jail in a minute, even if he could now pay off the mafia and maybe use the money to save his life. I wouldn't begrudge him that.

I had one thing in mind and one thing only. And it wasn't buying a pair of shoes or even another car. I ran my thumb along the stitching of Jordan's number on the back of the heel, felt the Jumpman logo stitched into the leather. The thinness of the raised arm, topped by the ball, the feet spread as if walking—on air—and the trail arm hanging down by his side. The thread felt smooth, soft.

I hadn't had a chance to try them on.

59

Top of the World

"Bye, Mike," I said to nobody in particular.

Then I turned and followed the others out of Trump's inner sanctuary and to the elevator.

We all three got on, and I knew it was only a matter of time before Gina and Mody started talking about the money, what the split should be and what they meant to do with it.

Outside the elevator, all of Central Park and New York City stretched out below us, from The Bronx down to Lady Liberty. We could see it all, so much of this high-priced, exclusive, precious world. From this high up, it looked pristine. I could almost believe I was on top of it all. So I rolled the dice, took my shot to go after what I really wanted, the thing that I had been pining for all along, even if I didn't know it until then.

I reached my arms around Mody and Gina's shoulders, pulled them closer to me. "Guys," I said, "how about the three of us go out to Hollywood and make a movie?"

JOIN THE FAMILY

Did you enjoy this book? Want another for FREE?

Without the power of a big publisher's budget behind my books, I rely on the power of a few good readers... **a committed and loyal bunch called... the Palms Mommas and the Palms Daddies. Together we can change the world!**

Use this link or visit sethharwood.com/family to join. Follow the link to join and I'll send you another book in the series for FREE!

You'll also get updates about new releases, special content, info on my street team and audio podcasts, and much, much more!

I am eager and excited to hear from you!

Sign up now!

REVIEWS

Honest reviews help bring this book to the attention of other readers.

If you've enjoyed this title, please spend just a few minutes leaving a review (it can be as short as you like) on the book's Amazon page. You can jump right to that page by visiting the URL below.

getbook.at/themaltesejordans

Thank you very much.

ALSO BY SETH HARWOOD
Have you read them all?

JACK PALMS CRIME

1
Jack Wakes Up

Washed-up movie star Jack Palms left Hollywood, kicked his drug habit, and played it as straight as anyone could ask for three years. Now the residual checks are drying up and the monastic lifestyle's starting to wear thin. When Jack tries to cash in on his former celebrity by showing some out-of-town high rollers around San Francisco's club scene, he finds himself knee-deep in a Bay Area drug war.

And the thing that scares Jack the most? He's starting to enjoy himself.

It'll take the performance of a lifetime to get him through it alive.

Buy it: getbook.at/jackwakesup

2
This Is Life

Jack finds himself in the middle of a whodunit in the seedy red-light district of San Francisco. Young girls, shipped as merchandise from Balkan countries and sold to city heavyweights, are turning up dead and no one knows why. Closer to home, a crooked cop steps out of Jack's past and into his backyard, taking potshots from the bushes at midnight.

Buy it: getbook.at/thisislife

3
Czechmate

Once hired by the SFPD to investigate the mysterious murder of a crooked cop, Jack Palms now finds himself in the path of Alexi Akakievich, a cruel drug lord with a ring of sex slaves tapped directly into the city's political elite.

What's unclear is whether Akakievich wants the power they can give him, or if he just wants to tear the city down. Whether Jack likes it or not, he finds himself in the way. Luckily, in Czechmate we see the return of Vlade, Niki and Al to stand by his side.

Buy it: getbook.at/czechmate

OR if you're curious about JUNIUS PONDS and want to read his origin story, you'll enjoy:

4
Young Junius

In 1987, Junius Posey sets out on the cold Cambridge (MA) streets to find his brother's killer in a cluster of low-income housing towers—prime drug-dealing territory. After committing a murder to protect himself and his friend, he finds himself without protection from retribution. Shocked by the violence he's created and determined to see its consequences through to their end, he returns to the towers to complete his original mission.

Buy it: getbook.at/youngjunius

JESS HARDING, FBI

In Broad Daylight

During the endless days of an Alaskan summer, a fiend slashes his way through the rural community, where everyone knows your name and always distrusts the outsider. FBI agent Jess Harding treks back to Anchorage to hunt down this sadistic killer who's reemerged from a five-year hiatus—a killer who has already slipped from her grasp once before.

As Jess attempts to immerse herself in the area's culture, she finds a strange rural village inhabited by Russian Old Believers hell-bent on protecting their way of life. Soon Jess needs a safehaven from the glare of daylight—a blood-stained message left at the scene of a murder says she's no longer the hunter, but the hunted.

Buy it: getbook.at/inbroaddaylight

CLARA DONNER, SFPD HOMICIDE

Everyone Pays

Detective Clara Donner worked vice in San Francisco for years alongside the runaways and vulnerable women who walk the night. She thinks she's seen the worst people can do—until she's assigned to investigate a particularly ruthless serial killer.

As the body count rises and a pattern emerges—each victim is known for his brutal abuse of women—Donner follows the killer's trail across the city. In spite of a nagging sense that the world may be better off without these men, that maybe this killer is doing good, she pursues every lead… until she finds a damaged girl with links to both the killer and his prey. Is this new witness the key to unraveling these murders or another victim left in the killer's wake?

Buy it: getbook.at/everyonepays

Short Stories

A Long Way from Disney

Do you like short stories?

This collection will blow you away.

You'll love this book because it will make you remember, laugh, even cry.

Divorced parents. A fractured family. Adam Berkman navigates his adolescence the best he can. Among Top 40 hits. Chicken McNuggets. First dances. First dates. Nintendo. Even into college and beyond.

You'll love how the relationship troubles of the son follow those of his parents and seeing if he can get through, get past it all to be happy. As he becomes a man.

Get it now and start reading.

Buy it: getbook.at/longwaydisney

Fisher Cat and Other Stories

Fisher Cat and other stories goes beyond the boundaries of adolescence and into the seeds of modern-day manhood in America.

From learning to capture the troublesome animal in the Dumpster, to dealing with the events of 9/11, confronting birth, babies, marriage and beyond, these stories take readers on a tour of the human heart—its foibles, failings and frangible pieces—on the streets of Pamplona, Spain, New York City, Boston, and points afar.

Buy it: getbook.at/fishercat

ABOUT THE AUTHOR

Seth Harwood is the author of the bestsellers *Everyone Pays, In Broad Daylight,* and *Jack Wakes Up,* as well as *Young Junius* and *This Is Life.*

He received an MFA from the Iowa Writers' Workshop and teaches creative writing at Harvard Extension as well as Stanford Continuing Studies. He lives in Western Massachusetts. Find more and contact him online at sethharwood.com and patreon.com/sethharwood. He loves to hear from readers.

44393030R00201

Made in the USA
Middletown, DE
10 May 2019